The Stage Manager's Handbook

By Bert Gruver
Revised by Frank Hamilton

Drama Book Publishers
New York

Library of Congress Catalog Card Number: 72-190641
ISBN: 0-89676-007-3

CONTENTS

FOREWORD TO FIRST EDITION

A textbook on stage managing would be a monumental work, running to several volumes, because the stage manager's duties touch all production departments. Actually there is no need for such a book, since the bulk of it would be a duplication of material found in standard books on the theater. If the newcomer to Broadway is familiar with these standard books, or with such basic technique as he might acquire in a college drama department, a good summer of little theater, or a professional school, he will not require a textbook on stage managing. However, he may need a guidebook to help him utilize his basic knowledge in the stage manager's special field. This handbook has been written to supply that guide, and it should help the reader augment or consolidate his knowledge in terms of the Broadway production. A subtitle might be "A Method of Procedure for the Stage Manager of the Broadway or Touring Legitimate Play."

The stage manager's procedure, what his duties are, will be listed in detail. How he accomplishes those duties will be explained or illustrated only when standard books on the theater have ignored or neglected them. The *how's* are illustrative and must not be construed as being definitive. There is no limit to how a stage manager accomplishes his work except the limitations of the production itself and the extent of the stage manager's ingenuity.

FOREWORD TO THE REVISED EDITION

A whole generation of stage managers has cut its teeth on Bert Gruver's book. These stage managers are now practicing their profession in the New York theatre. They all have their own, often highly individualistic, ways of doing things. But for the basis of their skills they usually owe a huge debt of gratitude to Bert Gruver.

An attempt to revise what is by now a classic shows a certain amount of gall. However, the last version was finished in 1953 and times do change. Union rules change, techniques change, and, to an extent, the function of the stage manager changes.

What doesn't change is Mr. Gruver's respect for the theatre. The obvious love he lavished on his profession shows through in page after page.

Where the original is more or less subjective (e.g., the section on casting) it has not been changed. Where it deals with facts and figures which must become out-of-date, those have been changes. Where it deals with methods some difficult choices have been made. Some of Mr. Gruver's methods are, or have become, standard practice. Others (while not necessarily the revisor's) are good, solid ways of doing things and have been kept. Others are no longer considered standard and have been changed.

Where the new edition fails to come up to the mark set by Bert Gruver's original, the revisor takes full blame. Where it clarifies and brings the original up-to-date without losing Bert Gruver's tone, the revisor acknowledges his own debt of gratitude to Mr. Gruver.

Frank Hamilton

INTRODUCTION

The production of a play may be likened to the manufacture of any complicated article. The various parts are created separately, are brought together at the proper time by careful planning and scheduling, and are assembled into a complete unit. After testing, the product is presented to the public.

The pre-rehearsal weeks and the first weeks of rehearsal are a period for planning and for starting the manufacture of the units of the production. The final rehearsal weeks see the beginning of assembly. During the set-up and technical rehearsals the final assembly takes place. The dress rehearsal and try-out tour are the testing, and the New York opening is the presentation of the finished product to the public.

During this time the talents, time and energies of many specialists are applied to the product. The playwright, the director, the actor, the choreographer, the designer, the stage hand all ply their specialties, as does the stage manager.

The stage manager's specialty is not "creative" in the sense that the author's or composer's is. However, if the stage manager has done his job well, the satisfaction he receives is second to no one's involved in the production. And his feeling for the finished product is usually intensely possessive. A stage manager who is incapable of a "love affair" with a show would do better to seek calmer and more profitable employment in a different profession.

A casual and generally accepted definition of the stage manager is one who has "charge of everything backstage." This is literally true. However, the stage manager is more than a foreman in charge of the producer's backstage employees.

A somewhat more formal definition of the duties of a stage manager has been developed by Actors' Equity Association for the guidance of stage managers and producers:

A Stage Manager under Actors' Equity Contract is, or shall be, obligated to perform at least the following duties for the Production to which he is engaged, and by performing them is hereby defined as the Stage Manager:

1. He shall be responsible for the calling of all rehearsals, whether before or after opening.
2. He shall assemble and maintain the Prompt Book, which is defined as the accurate playing text and stage business, together with such cue sheets, plots, daily records, etc., as are necessary for the actual technical and artistic operation of the production.
3. He shall work with the Director and the heads of all other departments during rehearsal and after opening, schedule rehearsal and outside calls in accordance with Equity's regulations.
4. He shall assume active responsibility for the form and discipline of rehearsal and performance, and be the executive instrument in the technical running of *each* performance.
5. He shall maintain the artistic intentions of the Director and the Producer after opening, to the best of his ability, including calling correctional rehearsals of the company when necessary, and the preparation of the Understudies, Replacements, Extras and Supers, when and if the Director and/or the Producer declines this prerogative.
6. He shall keep such records as are necessary to advise the Producer on matters of attendance, time, welfare benefits, or other matters relating to the rights of Equity members. *The Stage Manager and Assistant Stage Managers are prohibited from the making of payrolls or the distribution of salaries.*
7. He shall maintain discipline, as provided in the Equity Constitution, By-Laws and Rules where required, appealable in every case to Equity.
8. The Council shall have the power from time to time to define the meaning of the words "Stage Manager" and may alter, change or modify the meaning of Stage Manager as hereinabove [sic] defined.
9. The Stage Manager and Assistant Stage Managers are prohibited from handling contracts, having riders signed or initialed, or any other function which normally comes under the duties of the General Manager or Company Manager.

10. The Stage Manager and the Assistant Stage Managers are prohibited from participating in the ordering of food for the company.
11. The Stage Manager and the Assistant Stage Managers shall be prohibited from signing the closing notice of the company or the individual notice of an Actor on termination of contract.

While this definition is accurate, it is also extremely general. And it is one-sided—seen from the point of view of Actors' Equity Association and written in the literary style which only labor unions seem able to master.

For a broader view of the stage manager's function, let us look at the organization and work of the other specialists in the theatre. Almost all personnel are members of unions and a simplified chart of their organization follows.

INDEPENDENT ASSOCIATIONS

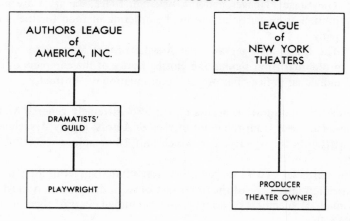

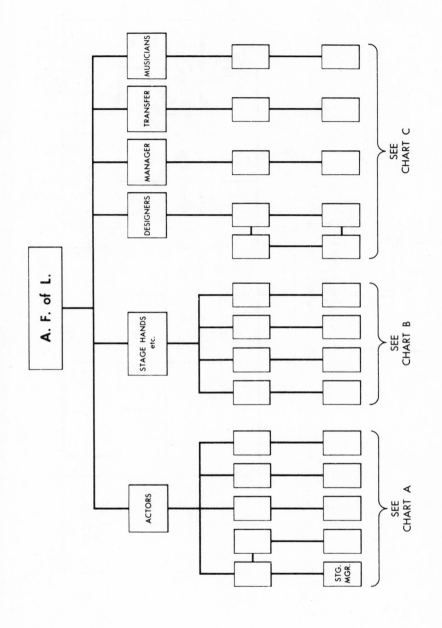

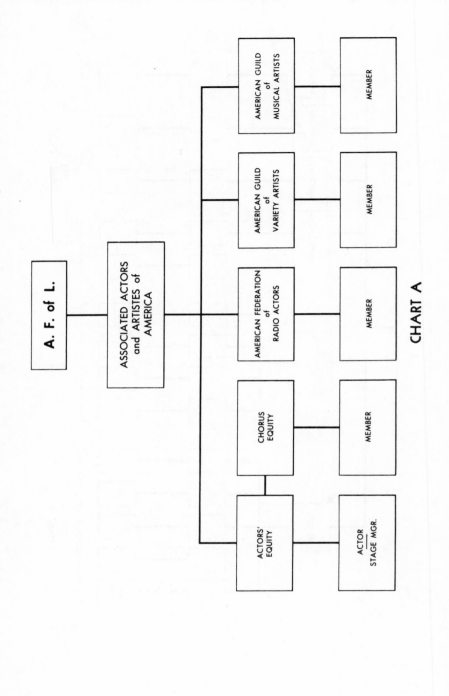

CHART A

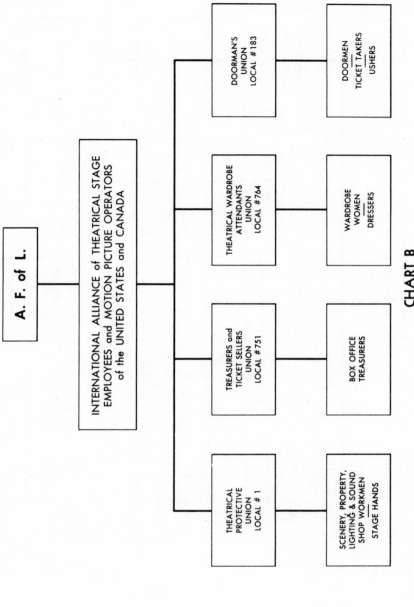

CHART B

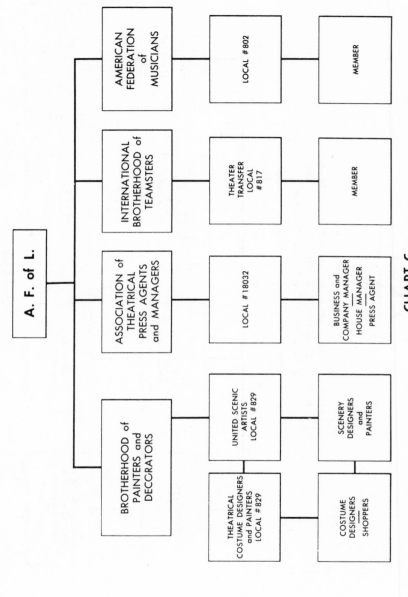

A. F. of L.

| BROTHERHOOD of PAINTERS and DECORATORS | ASSOCIATION of THEATRICAL PRESS AGENTS and MANAGERS | INTERNATIONAL BROTHERHOOD of TEAMSTERS | AMERICAN FEDERATION of MUSICIANS |

THEATRICAL COSTUME DESIGNERS and PAINTERS LOCAL #829

UNITED SCENIC ARTISTS LOCAL #829

LOCAL # 18032

THEATER TRANSFER LOCAL #817

LOCAL #802

COSTUME DESIGNERS
SHOPPERS

SCENERY DESIGNERS and PAINTERS

BUSINESS and COMPANY MANAGER
HOUSE MANAGER
PRESS AGENT

MEMBER

MEMBER

CHART C

Each union binds its members by laws and regulations which, in turn, govern the stage manager's actions.

The work of the other specialists (which will also govern the stage manager's actions) can be briefly described as follows:

The Producer:

The boss—he has charge of everything.

The General Manager:

The producer's right hand. Handles all financial details such as contracts, expenditures, budgets, etc.

The Playwright:

Writes the play and furnishes or approves all changes to it. Approves all actors and sometimes the director.

The Composer:

Composes the music. Works closely with the playwright and lyricist on the over-all concept. Supervises all music in the show.

The Lyricist:

Writes lyrics to the songs. Works closely with the composer and playwright on the over-all concept.

The Director:

Directs the play. Approves all actors and all parts of the production.

The Choreographer:

Creates dances and supervises all dance movement.

The Conductor:

Conducts orchestra during performance. Often selects musicians. Rehearses soloists and/or chorus singers.

The Contractor:

Is responsible for hiring of orchestra members.

Dance Arranger:

Works closely with choreographer. Adapts music to choreography.

Orchestrator:

Orchestrates music. Develops composer's ideas orchestrally.

Dance Captain:

Notates choreography during rehearsal. (Sometimes acts as assistant choreographer.) Is responsible for maintainence of dance performances and training replacements.

Designer(s):

Designs all settings, costumes, lighting and properties subject to the approval of the producer, director and playwright. Supervises the execution of his designs.

Company Manager:

The general manager's representative for a particular production, especially at the theatre and when on tour.

Advance Agent:

An advance publicity man for extended out-of-town tryouts and productions on tour.

Press Agent:

The New York publicity man. (Sometimes the same as the advance agent.)

Production Stage Crew:

Carpenter. Supervises original setup of scenery and, there-after is in charge of handling and maintenance of scenery. He is the traditional "head" of the production stage crew and, consequently, head man of all stage hands.

Property Man. Aids designer in procurement, collection and preparation of properties. Thereafter is in charge of their handling and maintenance.

Electrician. Aids designer by preparing and collecting lighting equipment, effects and fixtures. Thereafter is in charge of handling, maintenance and operation of lighting equipment.

Wardrobe Mistress. Aids designer in procurement, collection and preparation of costumes. Is in charge of handling and maintaining them.

Sound Operator. Aids in procurement and collection of sound equipment and effects. Maintains and operates it.

Scenic Artist (Retouch Man):

A member of the scenic studio staff who retouches or repaints scenery in the theatre.

Production Secretary:
Often the director's private secretary, sometimes the manuscript typist.

Miscellaneous:
The following personnel may be encountered; their titles explain their functions: Actors' Agent, Casting Director, Music Copyist, Office Secretary, Office Typist, Accountant, Sound Technician.

The stage manager comes in constant contact with all of these specialists. Sometimes, indeed, he is the only member of the production to deal with *all* of them. The stage manager is often spoken of as being the "center" of the production. And, to be sure, he is. This is not to say that ·he is the inspiration for the production. The inspiration remains the playwright's manuscript. Also, in producing a play, there is someone whose spark gives life and design to the production. This giver-of-the-spark, this animator or inspiritor, may be the producer, the director, the playwright, or the production's star. He is never the stage manager! The stage manager is the center of the production in the sense that he functions as liaison among all the production departments. As such, he should have a knowledge of the "nuts and bolts" of the other specialties. He may not know a quarter-note from an oboe, but he should know in general how the orchestrator accomplishes his work, in terms of time. He may not have the faintest notion of how to tie a spanish bowline, but he must be able to grasp a master carpenter's explanation of a proposed short-cut and to discern how it will affect the artistic function of the show.

We have seen that a stage manager's job is one of command ("has charge of everything backstage") and one of liaison. Add one futher, and most important, element: he is the translator of ideas into realities. How he accomplishes these tasks will be seen in the sections of the handbook, which follow the development of the production of a play: the planning and creating of the units, the assembling, the testing, and the presentation to the public.

The Stage Manager's Handbook

PART ONE

Prerehearsal Period

THE MANUSCRIPT

The manuscript of a new play is its mainspring, the source of all ideas and activity. It will be one of the first things the stage manager meets in his new job, and from it he will determine his future action.

I. Filing and Recording. The stage manager is one of the first to come in contact with the manuscript of a new play. It will be his most important duty to preserve and expand this manuscript. As Actors' Equity does not permit a stage manager to work except at full salary, he often does not start work earlier than two weeks before the first rehearsal. This is what he will find: There will have been one or several "editions" of the play already typed and the copies scattered among the playwright, producer, director, designers, potential backers, and actors. Depending on the size of the producer's office staff, there may or may not be an accurate file record of the manuscripts. The stage manager should see that there is such a file, setting it up and keeping it himself if necessary. The file includes this information:

1. Copy identification - edition date and number.
2. To whom each copy is issued and date.

Each time sufficient changes in the manuscript are made to require fresh typing, a new "edition" comes into being. The first extant edition may be identified by "A" and the copies by "A1," "A2," "A3," and so on. Identifying numbers and the date of typing of the edition should be place on the title page of each copy.

It is desirable to have each edition mimeographed. Mimeographed editions come in lots of twenty-five or more copies and are fairly costly (about $1.50 per copy, as an average). So, care must be taken that each edition is approved by the playwright, producer and director before being sent to the mimeographer.

When the mimeographed edition is received back, the stage manager should make sure that it is proofread, filed and recorded and that copies of the new script are placed in the hands of the appropriate personnel.

3

At this point it is profitable to make a "distribution list" of personnel requiring new editions or substantial revisions. It might read as follows:

Producer
Author
Director
Stage Manager
Assistant Stage Manager
Designer
Costume Designer
Lighting Designer
Composer
Lyricist
Choreographer
Dance Arranger
Actors

A copy of the distribution list should be left with the office secretary or production secretary, or whoever assumes the job of keeping track of the scripts. This job is usually better left in the hands of the producer's office personnel, as the producer's office is usually a permanent facility (as opposed to rehearsal halls) and has space for twenty-five or fifty manuscripts.

If the production is a musical, the stage manager should insist that lyrics be typed on a separate page in the mimeographed editions. Because lyrics are often rewritten independently of dialogue, and vice-versa, this will save much retyping later on.

The stage manager should see that no replaced scene or portion of dialogue and stage direction is discarded or lost. As removed, these portions can be filed with identifying notes, such as "Removed from Edition C, Act II, page 8, Oct. 10th." In time this may appear to be a collection of waste paper, but many occasions arise to justify its existence. Some playwrights insist that a copy of all discarded material be returned to them. Often it is decided to return to a version of a scene discarded weeks before. The stage manager is expected to have a copy. This collection of discards may be destroyed only after the New York opening of the play and then only after permission is received from both the playwright and the producer.

II. Editing and Typing. The stage manager must make sure that scripts are in the hands of the actors, the director and the stage managers by the first rehearsal. Actors playing small roles need not have a complete script. Pages may be taken from one script to supply scenes for several smaller roles, or pages may be reproduced by Xerox or they may be typed. Often, however, actors playing small roles will be understudying larger roles and they should be provided with a complete script.

The stage manager should establish who has the responsibility for typing, copying and distributing revisions. The author and lyricist should be made aware of the process by which their revisions are reproduced and distributed, and to whom they should give new material to be reproduced. In smaller productions, this may be a member of the stage management staff; in larger productions where the stage managers may be burdened with other work, it may be the office secretary or the production secretary.

In musical productions, where a great many rewrites may be expected, it may be desirable to rent a portable mimeograph machine and place it in the hands of the production secretary, whose principal duty it will be to keep track of rewrites and distribution. In all cases the desideratum is to keep all scripts as accurate as possible and to distribute rewrites to the proper personnel as rapidly as possible.

III. Planning the Performance Pattern. The ultimate goal of the professional theatre is the presentation of a play before a paying audience. When the stage manager reads and studies the manuscript, he thinks in terms of the performance and the form it will assume. This form, this scheme for organizing and managing the performance, this shape or plan of what happens during the performance, is called the *performance pattern* in this handbook. If the play to be produced is one of Shakespeare's, the pattern will be considerably different from the pattern for *Abie's Irish Rose*. The stage manager, along with other members of the production staff, determines this pattern by a study of the manuscript.

5

The first business of the stage manager, obviously, is to read the play. This first reading, or indeed, the first several readings, should not be done with pencil in hand. The play should be read as a literary or dramatic work, much as a play might be read on a chilly evening for pure enjoyment. Since the stage manager will soon enough begin to think of the play as a series of elements or functions, that "first fine careless rapture" may not be entirely recaptured until after opening night. And, as will be seen, a stage manager must have an artistic understanding of the play. It is valuable to record subjective impressions at this time, adding to or revising these notes as the director or author expresses himself during the production period.

The stage manager will then begin the job which will occupy him daily until after the opening; that is, the preparing of the prompt script.

Since this prompt script will eventually be the heart of any production, care must be taken in its creation. The term *prompt script* is qualified by different people in different ways. The term *working prompt script* is often heard. This indicates that the speaker is referring to the stage manager's own script, which has been marked for use during the rehearsal or performance; while identical to other scripts insofar as dialogue is concerned, it will differ from them in many respects. The use of prompt script in this handbook will be all-inclusive. The reader should bear in mind that *(a)* the prompt script starts as a manuscript received from the playwright, without plots or other technical details; *(b)* during rehearsals, tryouts and up to opening night (and sometimes thereafter), the prompt script undergoes constant revision, elaboration, and inclusion of technical details; *(c)* it is brought into a finished state after the opening. If the reader remembers this, he should have no difficulty identifying the nature of the prompt script as he progresses through this handbook.

The stage manager now begins reading the script with a pencil in hand and a pad of paper by his side. This process is often called *breaking down the script*. He should read through the script very carefully, looking for technical problems or difficulties. He will probably wind up with dozens of questions. Do actors have exits on one side of the stage and entrances seconds later on the other side? Does a character appear in Los Angeles when he appeared in New York in the previous scene, ten minutes earlier? The stage manager is occupied here with finding problems, not in their solution. It is likely that the solution has already been found by the author, director or designer; but if not, they should be made aware that the problems exist. If, however, the solution to a problem presents itself, the stage manager should make note of it.

It is at this point that the *Plots* are begun. The plots are merely the isolating of the elements of the play into departmental or functional parts. The first organizing of this material is called the *Preliminary Plots* with the operative word being "preliminary."

The following plots should be started:

1. Actor Plot
2. Costume Plot
3. Carpentry Plot
4. Lighting Plot
5. Sound Plot
6. Property Plot

Information on these plots will only include elements found in the manuscript. If the stage direction reads: "Mary appears in a blue evening gown," it may be safely assumed that a blue evening gown is what Mary wears in the scene. "Herbert lights a cigarette," would appear on the Property Plot as: "Cigarettes—Herbert."

A. THE ACTOR AND COSTUME PLOTS. The preliminary actor plot should show the character's name and the scenes in which he appears. It can be combined with the preliminary costume plot as illustrated:

Char- acters	ACT I		ACT II	ACT III
	Scene 1 Living Room	Scene 2 Bedroom	Hunting Lodge	Living Room
JOHN	Dinner Jacket	1. Pajamas 2. Suit	Tweeds	1. Dinner Jacket 2. Smoking "
MARY	Evening Gown	Nightgown & Robe	1. Traveling Suit 2. Slacks, Jacket	Evening Gown (Blue)
ANN (Maid)	Uniform (Black)	Uniform (Same?)		Uniform?
JEEVES (Butler)	Uniform			Uniform
etc.	etc.	etc.	etc.	etc.

8

For a large cast, a multi-scene play or a musical, the stage manager should also make actor plots for each scene:

ACT I, Scene 3
72nd Street

Character	Actor	Understudy or Swing	Costume
Principals			
Joe	Smith	Hansen	Blue Suit
Fred	Jones	Peters	?
Chorus			
Organ Grinder	Hansen	Riorden	Pointed Hat Red Shirt
Gypsy	Elworth	?	Green Dress
Cop	Gelb	Riorden	1910 Uniform
Nanny	?	?	Nurse's Uniform

This plot, as the others, will develop as consultations are held regarding casting, understudying and costumes.

It may smack of caste system to separate the principals and chorus—not so! If, for example, the director wishes to rehearse the "dialogue" part of the scene at the same time the choreographer wishes to rehearse the dance number, this type of separation will prove invaluable to the stage manager when making the call.

B. THE CARPENTRY PLOT. At this point the carpentry plot will be little more than a listing of the scenes of the play. The stage manager should begin it, nonetheless. When completed (after consultation with the designer), the carpentry plot will indicate every scenic element in each scene plus methods for accomplishing changes.

ACT I
   Scene 1—Living Room
      Wagons A & B ON
      Blue Cyc. IN
      Turntable to Position "A"

9

Scene 2—Bedroom
Wagons A & B OFF
Wagon C ON
Turntable to Position "B"
Blue Cyc. IN

ACT II
Scene 1—Hunting Lodge
Wagons A & B ON (To be reset during intermission)
Blue Cyc. IN
Fog Scrim IN
Turntable to Position "C"

ACT III—Living Room
Wagons A & B ON (To be reset during intermission)
Blue Cyc. IN
Fog Scrim OUT
Turntable to Position "A"

Much of the information will not, of course, be included in the preliminary plot for the simple reason that it will not be known to the stage manager. Again, only information included in the text of the play or the stage directions should be included in the preliminary plots.

C. LIGHTING PLOT. The preliminary light plot (the "ing" in "lighting" is frequently dropped by theatre people) may be very simple or fairly elaborate, depending on the play; but, simple or not, it should be outlined.

ACT I		ACT II	ACT III
Scene 1 Living Room	Scene 2 Bedroom	Hunting Lodge	Living Room
Evening – Table lamps are light source – possible fading of light outside window – no special effects	Morning – Bright morning sunlight from windows – no special effects.	Afternoon – Warm afternoon sun through windows – no change or effects	Night – Thunder storm – lightning outside window – table lamps flicker, brighten, go out – candles used temporarily (electric candles?) lights on dim – brighten – snap off individually – fireplace flicker thruout scene

11

D. THE SOUND PLOT. The sound plot may be constructed in the same form as the light plot and should include all effects, no matter how trivial, with ample notes and descriptions.

From this preliminary plot the over-all requirements may be determined. Explicit dialogue for recordings will be supplied by the playwright and the director.

ACT I		ACT JI	ACT III
Scene I	Scene 2		
Telephone bell (Supply 2 Sets) etc.	NO EFFECTS	Automobile offstage approaching & stop, starting & leaving. (high-powered car) Voice calling in distance & echoing among hills (special recording ?) etc.	Thunder-all variations Practical telephone When used audience hears : Ringing at other end Busy signal Voices, male & female, not words etc.

Specifications

1. Automobile associated with Stage R.
2. Echoing voice comes from "all around" - actors cannot determine where caller is.
3. Thunder "all around."
4. Intercom system for stage manager controlled from prompt desk with 5 stations as follows:
   Station 1 - All stations hooked together
        "   2 - O.P. (Opposite Prompt side)
        "   3 - Upstage Center
        "   4 - Fly floor or pin rail
        "   5 - Switchboards
5. Special mike in foots leading to prompt desk to pick up cues (this may be extended to dressing rooms as monitor for actors).
6. Intercom between audience and switchboard for designer when lighting show.

        etc.   etc.

E. THE PROPERTY PLOT. The preliminary property plot need not be elaborately set up, but should be as complete in detail as possible. It should include all properties that are described by the author, either directly or indirectly—in the stage directions or by the characters in

12

their dialogue. Placement and arrangement of the properties will be
added to the prop list before the setup and dress rehearsals.

ACT I, Scene 1
Living Room

SET PROPS (Heavy or fixed props)

> Couch
> Table (fairly large)
> Table (bridge, folding)
> Armchair (large, solid back, actor hides behind it)
> Desk (special top - letter opener to be stuck into it)
> Practical roller window shade on window D.R.
> etc., etc.

SMALL PROPS (including décor when known, hand and personal props and
actor using them)

> Cigarette lighter (JOHN)
> Cigarette case (JOHN)
> Tray of 6 cocktail glasses, martinis (BUTLER), actors never drink
> Evening bag (Mary), must have compartment for revolver - COSTUMES
> Dial telephone handset on desk - practical - SOUND NOTE
> etc., etc.

ACT, I, Scene 2
Bedroom

SET PROPS

> Double bed, no footboard, reinforced three sides for sitting
> Dressing table
> Heavy drapes on window, practical draw type
> etc., etc.

SMALL PROPS

> Cigarette case (JOHN) conspicuously different from case Act I, Scene I
> Hand mirror on dressing table - pink plastic - long handle
> etc., etc.

ACTS II & III

etc.   etc.

Bear in mind that these are *preliminary* plots, which will undergo
change and elaboration during rehearsals and will develop into finished
plots after the play has opened. It is wise to title these plots
"preliminary" and to date them. When enough new material or
information has been accumulated to warrant retyping of the plots,
they, too, should be dated. The stage manager will have to use his best

13

judgment in making a new "edition" of a plot. When, in rehearsal, the director says, "I want a low table to be placed here," the information can be hand-written on the property plot without making an entirely new plot (making sure the information is passed on quickly to the designer and the property man.) When the director has requested enough additional tables, chairs, cupboards, ottomans, credenzas and antimacassars, and the stage manager's copy of the property plot begins to look as if it had been walked upon by a hen with inky feet, it is obviously time to make a new edition of the property plot.

While the end result of these plots is to be historical, that is, the finished prompt script from which an identical production of the play could be produced, the *immediate* use of these plots is informational. A collection of the most accurate and complete plots in a stage manager's briefcase is of little use if it remains in his briefcase. Only when they are in the hands of the proper personnel and are understood will they justify the considerable work the stage manager has gone to in making them.

IV. Activating the Plots. The stage manager must now begin to think in terms of accomplishing the requirements of the script. Even though his information is incomplete, he must now begin planning the performance pattern. This planning will continue through the opening, and as each new element is added to the play it will become a part of the plan. If the plan is well conceived, the new element will fit in with little problem.

To this end, the stage manager will begin to think in terms of *cues*. A cue is merely a sequence, either visual or aural. If, in the script Character A speaks and then Character B speaks, the cue for Character B to speak is the last word of A's speech. If, after Character B speaks, the telephone rings, the cue for the telephone is the end of B's speech.

The reader may wonder why cuing, primarily a performance duty, is discussed in detail now. It must be realized that one of the most important functions of the stage manager is *to anticipate*. The producer will expect his stage manager to foresee the problems in the interlocking of the production elements, and to develop solutions during this planning period. Now is the time to alter or adjust the

14

production elements to fit the ultimate pattern. Later, during the assembling and testing periods loss of time will be wasteful and expensive. The stage manager must study the manuscript thoroughly and develop a pattern of performance built upon interlocking cues.

Cues divide themselves easily into two types, direct and indirect.

A. DIRECT CUES. Most of the performance cues will be direct cues. Each word of dialogue is, in a sense, a cue for the succeeding word. An actor, waiting outside an entrance, hears another actor say a particular word; then the first actor enters. He has received a direct cue. A follow-spot operator watches an actor enter and brings on his follow-spot on the actor. The follow-spot operator has received a direct business cue. He has also received a *sight cue*. These direct cues constitute the bulk of the play and will take care of themselves. The stage manager determines that the giver and receiver of the cue understood that it is a direct cue and stands by to assist if necessary, but he can presume that once learned, it will be accomplished automatically.

B. INDIRECT CUES. The stage manager will sort out from all cues those that cannot be received automatically and directly. These will need an intermediary or relay to get the impulse from the source to the receiver. This relay is often the stage manager himself; or, he may be the supervising agent, overseeing personnel or mechanical relays.

To accomplish these indirect cues the stage manager will have two types of equipment: the fixed equipment found in the theatre, and the special equipment that the stage manager devises and has the production furnish.

1. Fixed Equipment. Every theatre furnishes some permanent cuing equipment, usually built into the theatre at the time of its construction. This equipment varies greatly in elaborateness and usefulness from theatre to theatre but generally includes: signals to dressing rooms, signal to the stage hands' room, signal to the orchestra pit, signal to the orchestra greenroom, curtain signal, and lobby signal. The stage manager can expect to find these systems in varying forms and degrees of repair and usefulness. All other necessary cuing devices will be planned by the stage manager and furnished by the production.

15

2. Portable (or Production-furnished) Equipment. Of the cuing equipment that the production may furnish, personnel is the most important. By utilizing personnel to relay the cue, the stage manager eliminates the outstanding drawback to the other cuing systems: mechanical failure. Personnel generally use voice or hand cues which consist of a warning, a ready, and a go. The warning should be given sufficiently in advance of the ready to allow the receiver time to make last-minute preparations. The ready and go come fairly close together. The warning may be given by voice or some other means. The arm raised over the head is the ready, and the arm dropped to the side is the go. Or, if the cue is given entirely by voice (in a case where the receiver is out of view of the relayer) it might be given as follows:

Warn Electrics (Cue) Five—The electrician glances at his cue book, checks that the proper switches are on and the proper dimmer handles are locked.

Electrics Five—The electrician has his hands on the dimmer handles.

Go—The electrician executes the cue.

Light-cue systems usually consist of a pilot light and switch at the prompt desk, and a cue light at the point where the cue is to be received. The light on means ready; the light off means go. These light systems are often wired in series; a disadvantage, because a burned-out pilot light means a dead cue light. Should this happen during the giving of a cue, confusion and error will result. Wiring the system in parallel, with two bulbs at the cue-receiving end, will largely eliminate this problem.

Increased efficiency has brought intercommunication systems more and more into favor as a means of giving cues and as a monitor in dressing rooms and corridors. Their advantages are several: the spoken word will attract attention when a light may not; interlocking systems allow the stage manager to give cues individually to distant stations or collectively to several or all stations (a flexibility most light systems do not have); in case of mishap the stage manager can carry on a conversation with distant points; and any one outlet can be used for various departments or functions by using a single introductory word such as "Props!" or "Actors!"

16

A microphone pickup in the footlights leading to a monitor on the prompt desk is valuable both in very quiet scenes and in scenes where there is a great deal of offstage noise.

Intercom systems have their drawbacks. Mechanical failure is an obvious one, and so there must be an alternative, independent system of some type standing by. In very quiet plays voice cues are dangerous and an intercom system is used sparingly or the cue receivers are provided with "hearing aid" type of receivers or head-sets (an additional expense!). Monitors in dressing rooms may lead to indifference on the actor's part. One may become so familiar with the ticking and hourly striking of a clock that one ignores it. The same can happen with a monitor.

The cuing system developed for any given production is most often a combination of intercom system, light-cue system and hand signals. One of the main points to be considered by the stage manager in determining the cuing systems to be used is the "fail-safeness" of the setup. Will he be able to continue to activate the cues if a malfunction occurs?

If the play is a relatively simple one, the stage manager may be able to determine his equipment needs at this point. If so, he should make a list of the equipment needed and include it in the light plot, making sure that the lighting designer and the master electrician understand it.

V. Preparing Prompt Script for Rehearsals. During the weeks before the first rehearsal the manuscript will have been brought into a working edition by the playwright and the director and is usually retyped and mimeographed. If the stage manager has been using an early edition for his preliminary work, he will abandon it and replace it with the new edition, making sure to include any new information in the plots. He will also make sure that his assistants have the latest edition and, if available, it is wise to take one or two copies as a reserve.

To be ready for the first rehearsal, the stage manager should make the following preparations of the manuscript:

   A. REBIND THE SCRIPT. Remove the brass paper fasteners and insert the loose pages in a spring-backed, rigid binder. These binders are known in the stationery trade as loose sheet holders.

This protects the script with a sturdy cover, prevents dog-earing and tearing of pages, and forms a background on which to write when not at a table. Some stage managers prefer to use loose-leaf binders which have rings and holes in the paper. This permits pages to be removed more easily and is of value in complicated productions where extensive revisions can be anticipated.

B. INSERT OPPOSITE EACH PAGE A SHEET OF 8½" X 11" TYPEWRITER PAPER (SAME SIZE AS MANUSCRIPT). These sheets serve as a handy note pad, and as additional space for recording stage directions and inserted dialogue. The sheets may be removed when prompting starts, for they may confuse the prompter. Blank sheets should be placed in the back of the book also, for day-to-day notes and reminder pads. They can be torn out at the end of each day and the notes transferred to a clip-board or other more organized notation system.

C. INDEX THE SCRIPT WITH TABS, ONE FOR EACH SCENE. In a multi-scene play individual scenes are often referred to by number—Act One, Scene 1 is 11 (eleven), Act One, Scene 2 is 12 (twelve), Act Two, Scene 1 is 21 (twenty-one), Act Three, Scene 1 is 31 (thirty-one). Appropriate scene numbers should be put on the tabs.

D. MARK THE CUES AND THE ACTORS' ENTRANCES IN THE SCRIPT. At the beginning of each scene a list of actors in that scene should be made and can be divided as follows:

At Rise:
Onstage: JOHN
             MARY
Ready Off: BUTLER
             MAID
Later: POSTMAN
             MARTHA

At a glance it is evident that when the scene starts JOHN and MARY must be onstage. The BUTLER and MAID must be ready for immediate entrances in the order listed, and during the scene the POSTMAN and MARTHA will enter in that order.

18

It is customary to precede each cue by a warning, usually one or more minutes of dialogue or stage business before the actual cue. One manuscript page is approximately one minute. This warning is marked in the right margin of the manuscript, e.g. WARN POSTMAN or WARN PHONE. A page or so later in the right margin opposite the cue word in the dialogue, which should be underscored, should be marked POSTMAN or PHONE. When a cue occurs at the top of a page a notation of some kind may be made on the preceding page so that the cue will not be missed while turning the page.

Some years ago it was practice to use various colored pencils to indicate the recipient of the cue—Red for electrics, green for sound, cerise for actors, and to draw lines in the proper colors from the warn to the go. Any stage manager who has tried to erase colored pencil markings knows this is not a good system. Since revision is "the name of the game" in many productions, an eraser is as important a piece of equipment as a pencil to a stage manager and "neatness counts." Plain black pencil is the most erasable way of marking a script and, if it is kept sharp, the neatest way. The ideal working prompt script is one from which any competent, well-trained stage manager could run a show, without having seen it before. This ideal is never reached, but it's something to shoot at.

An attempt should be made to give warnings and cues—especially those that result in backstage movement, and preparation—during audience laughs or action on the stage, e.g., to call the stage hands onto the stage for a scene shift not only in sufficient time for them to prepare themselves but during a portion of the scene when the arrival backstage of ten or twenty people will not disturb the performance. No matter how careful they are, ten people cannot avoid making some noise.

E. BE SURE TO PUT THE NAMES AND ADDRESSES OF THE PRODUCER AND STAGE MANAGER IN THE PROMPT SCRIPT. Heaven help the stage manager who loses his script!

19

Having made the above preparations, the stage manager's script is ready for rehearsals. During rehearsals and tryout performances, changes and additions to the script will be made. There are as many different methods of accumulating, tabulating, organizing and recording the material that will go into a prompt script as there are stage managers. Each stage manager will have his preferred system, but will find it necessary to alter it to fit the demands of a particular production. Whatever his system, the stage manager will keep in mind the elements a completed prompt script must contain, and will add them as they are developed during the rehearsal period.

The completed prompt script is not the manuscript as received from the playwright, or the one the reading public gets from the publisher. The first is lacking in technical details, and the latter is elaborated with descriptive material to help the reader visualize the physical production and understand the written word. The finished prompt script is a record of a play's production elements, and it is a guide to a method of bringing those elements into existence on a stage. With the single exception of the playwright's dialogue, which is preserved accurately, the prompt script is not a literary achievement.

The finished prompt script contains:

    a. Introduction:
      1. Title Page
      2. Lists of Casts of Characters and the Scenes.
      3. A copy of the opening night program.
      4. A full-stage picture of each set or a small-scale ground plan of each set, or both.

    b. The Play:
      1. Complete dialogue.
      2. Complete stage directions, including each actor's business, using traditional stage symbols or conventional abbreviations.
      3. Short, instructive mood or character directions such as, "tearfully," "happily," etc. The playwright will amplify these for the reading public; the stage manager will not, except when the meaning is not self-evident in the context.

4. Brief descriptions of the settings, including placement of important furniture, doors, windows, stairs, etc.
c. *The Technical Plots:*
1. Carpentry Plot—includes types of scenery and how they are handled in the shifts.
2. Property Plot—a brief but complete identifying description of every property and its placement on- or offstage.
3. Lighting Plot—complete listing of all equipment and its placement and purpose. A list of all light cues.
4. Costume Plot—complete list in detail of all costumes for each actor, including accesories and unusual make-up.
5. Sound Plot—list of equipment, including records and effects, and all cues.

GENERAL MANAGER AND STAGE MANAGER

One of the first members of the staff the stage manager meets is the producer's general (or business) manager. This may be the producer himself. The general manager will help pave the way for appointments with other staff members and will decide the firms the stage manager will deal with (typing agency, sound equipment company).

At this discussion the stage manager will also find out, if it is not known to him, who the other members of the staff are. He will save time for the general manager and himself if he prepares for this meeting with the general manager by making a list of every element of the production that is unknown to him.

I. Production Schedule. Between them, the general manager and the stage manager will discuss the over-all production schedule, including:
1. Date of first rehearsal.
2. Length of rehearsals (number of days).
3. Places to rehearse. As these are limited and must be reserved in advance, this schedule should be as complete as possible.
4. Date and place of scenery setup. Does the studio construction and painting the scenery make provision for the actors to see it in the studio before the stage setup?
5. Date of technical rehearsals.

6. Date of dress rehearsals.
7. Dates and places of out-of-town tryouts.
8. When and where will photos of the actors in costume and in the settings be taken?
9. When will the production heads of the stage crews be hired? Who are they? An experienced stage manager's suggestions are appreciated.
10. When during the rehearsal period will it be possible to hire a property man so that props may be used?

From the information he receives in this meeting the stage manager will make a *Production Schedule*—a chronological listing of the important events of the production.

SARAH'S OTHER HUSBAND
Production Schedule

Sept. 17, 19**

Oct. 4	First rehearsal—Judson Hall
Oct. 10	Company day off
Oct. 11-17	Company rehearse—Judson Hall (Day off during week to be determined.)
Oct. 18-24	Company rehearse—Judson Hall (Day off during week to be determined.)
Oct. 22	Production loads out of New York to Boston.
Oct. 23	Production begins take-in Wilber Theatre—Boston
Oct. 24	Production continue setup—Boston (Should begin focusing by evening.)
Oct. 25	Company: Travel to Boston (Company onstage: 8PM) Production: Finish focusing and lighting show. Prepare for company onstage 8 PM—No costumes.
Oct. 26	Production: 8-12 Tech clean-up—Finish lighting. 1-6 Tech run-thru (Stop and start)— Costumes. Costumes ready at 12:30. 7-12 Continue tech run-thru.

22

	Company:	12:30-5:30 Tech run-thru. Costumes.
		7-12 Continue tech run-thru.
Oct. 27	Production:	8-12 Tech clean-up as needed.
		1-6 1st dress rehearsal (Costumes & Make-up).
		7-12 2nd dress rehearsal (Costumes & Make-up).
	Company:	12:30-5:30 1st dress rehearsal.
		7-12 2nd dress rehearsal.
Oct. 28	Production:	8-12 As needed.
		1-6 As needed.
		8 PM Half-hour for Boston opening.
	Company:	8 PM Half-hour for Boston opening.
		(Rehearse during day as needed.)

N.B. Production pictures to be taken Oct. 29 or 30—To be determined by press department.

N.B. 2. Boston engagement for four weeks. During that time company must receive one full day off. To be determined.

It will be noted that in the above schedule the technical rehearsal times for the company and production are slightly different. This is because the union rules for stage hands and actors are slightly different. Stage hands receive one hour for meal breaks and the hour is set—twelve to one, six to seven. Actors receive an hour-and-a-half. So, in the example, the actors are called at twelve-thirty (along with the wardrobe department) so that they may prepare for a one o'clock rehearsal. They will then be ready to start, having donned their costumes, at one o'clock when the crew returns from lunch. If the crew has had a morning call, it will be wise to utilize the last half-hour of that call to prepare for the afternoon rehearsal. At five-thirty the actors must be given a meal break, leaving a half-hour of the crew's time for "fixes" of things which have not been right at the afternoon rehearsal.

This schedule, like the stage manager's other paper work, should be distributed to the personnel involved as soon as possible. This, too, is a preliminary plot and may or may not meet the needs of the staff. After consultation with the director, designer, lighting designer, master carpenter, master electrician, changes may be made in the schedule to accomodate the anticipated technical requirements. It will be of value for the general manager and the stage manager to arrange a meeting of all the production staff in order to go over the production schedule. Out of this conference will come the final version of the schedule. (Although "final" is perhaps too strong a word. Unforeseen problems will most certainly arise and the schedule will have to be changed. The stage manager will show his improvisational mettle by having contingency plans, if for example, the scenery take-in is held up by bad weather.)

II. Assistant Stage Managers. The selection of assistant stage managers is one of the first matters to be taken up between the general manager and the stage manager. The nature of the production is the deciding factor in the selection. The size of scenery in the production, the number of cues and the number and type of the actors (since the first assistant in dramas and the second assistants in musicals invariably understudy) are elements that help determine the number and type of assistants. A general but safe rule for determining the number is: after the New York opening, the stage manager should be able to leave the backstage area and watch an entire performance from the audience with the assurance that the performance will be conducted efficiently during his absence. If he cannot do this, either the production is understaffed or the stage manager has poorly trained assistants.

Many producers permit the stage manager to pick his own assistants, particularly if the production is heavy. This situation is ideal because assistants familiar with the stage manager's methods may be selected, subject only to the approval of the director and the playwright as to their suitability as small-part and/or understudy actors.

When the stage manager is unable to pick his own assistants, he should request that those picked for him be put on salary as soon as possible before rehearsals start. Not only does the stage manager require their services, but he must learn their capacities before the pressure of rehearsals is upon them. The stage manager must divide his responsibilities. To do this he will find out which of his assistants is best

24

equiped to manage cues, or actors, or costumes, or other production details. If the production is a musical, it is wise to have one second assistant who is a member of the chorus. He will be able to transmit information to the stage manager from the choreographic rehearsals at which the stage manager may not be present.

Furthermore, it is essential that more than one stage manager be familiar with *all* the details of the stage manager's part of the production. The production of a play must not be interrupted by the loss of the stage manager owing to sickness or any other reason. Once the assistants are hired, the stage manager will keep them posted on all details of his work. *No stage manager worth his salt withholds any pertinent information concerning the production from his assistants. He has no "trade secrets"!*

III. Contract Information. The stage manager will receive from the general manager the following contract information:

1. The names of all cast members on pink (or chorus) contract and those on white (principal) contract who receive $250 per week or less.
2. The roles and/or understudies assigned by contract to each chorus member.

The first piece of information will enable him to keep accurate records of illnesses and sick leave due. Each cast member on pink contract and each principal receiving $250 per week or less is entitled to one day sick leave for each four weeks of employment. The producer will expect the stage manager to keep accurate records and to notify him when an actor has exceeded his sick leave.

The second piece of information should be tabulated on 3" x 5" cards, keeping an individual card for each actor. As the play is revised and rewritten, this information will change and the general manager (or company manager) will want to know this, as it will possibly change the payment to the actor.

As soon as the play is cast the stage manager should compose cast lists with the name of each actor and spaces following. These can be used for attendance, sick leave records, records of costume fittings, etc.

SARAH'S OTHER HUSBAND

ALLEN, C.										
BELDEN, L.										
CARPENTER, J.										
DONIZETTI, L.										
ELSTON, R.										
FRIAR, R.										
GABLER, M.										
HERZOG, C.										
IVERSON, C.										
JOHNSON, A.										
KRAUSS, M.										
LEAVITT, J.										
etc.										
etc.										
etc.										

26

The stenographic service employed will be happy to mimeograph fifty or so copies when they mimeograph the script.

At the end of each week the stage manager will prepare and submit to the company manager a payroll memorandum. This need not be elaborate, but it must be accurate. It is simply a digest of any payroll adjustments which must be made for the following week.

SARAH'S OTHER HUSBAND
Payroll Memorandum   w/e Nov. 21, 19**

1. Friar our 11/16 & 11/17—Not covered by sick leave.
2. Gabler assumed role of Nordquist 11/19 (four performances).
3. Leavitt assigned to understudy Nordquist (additional $5/wk.)
4. Iverson played for Friar 11/16 & 11/17—2 performances. Addition two-eighths of salary.

IV. Preparation of the Rehearsal Stage Floor. If the rehearsals are to be held in a theatre, the house property man and the house carpenter will have to be called (usually a four-hour call) when the stage manager marks the rehearsal stage with ground plans of the settings. If the rehearsals are to be held in a rehearsal hall the stage hands need not be called, but in either case, a time should be arranged when the rehearsal space is available to the stage manager to mark the stage. The complexity of the markings will depend upon the design of the production and whether the rehearsal space is permanent or temporary. If the rehearsals are to change from place to place, the stage manager should consider the use of a marked ground cloth. (This will constitute an expense and approval should be given by the general manager.) In general, the more simple the design, the more elaborate and detailed can be the rehearsal stage markings. A multi-set show may use different colored tapes for each set, and if the various sets are elaborately detailed, the stage floor becomes a rainbow of confusion to the actors and director.

V. Address List. It is important to compile an address list. This list should include the addresses and phone numbers of all persons connected with the production, including: actors, playwright, composer, lyricist, conductor, director, choreographer, producer (home phone), general manager (home phone), producer's office, designer's and assistants' office and home phones, stage managers, publicity agent, company manager, crew heads, shops (scenery, electrics, props, costumes), orchestra contractor, copyist, typing service, and any other specials. Most people prefer this to be a typed list on one sheet of paper that may be carried easily in the pocket. It should be dated and kept accurate. Copies should be given the producer, director, general manager, office secretary, company manager, each stage manager, each designer, press agent—but should not be given out indiscriminately, since the list often includes unlisted, private numbers. This list will grow and change daily and must be kept current. The general manager will furnish the material to start the address list; the stage manager will keep it current. The services of the office typist are enlisted when preparing an address list.

VI. Sound Equipment. Utilizing the preliminary sound plot the general manager and the stage manager will discuss sound equipment problems:

1. Types of effects required.
2. Amount and type of equipment to be used.
3. Intercommunication system for cuing.
4. Intercommunication system from stage to dressing rooms.
5. Special recordings to be made.
6. Releases for standard recordings.
7. Is a sound technician required? Who?
8. What firm will supply the equipment?
9. Has an operator been hired? Who?

VII. Music. If the production is to be a musical, the music department will be large, and most likely will be quite well organized before the stage manager is hired. The stage manager's obligation to the music department will be to make sure that rehearsal time and space are available. In his first conference with the general manager, he will find out how the music department is organized. Will the composer rehearse soloists? Will the conductor rehearse soloists? Will they share this duty?

Will a separate choral director be employed to rehearse the chorus? Et cetera . . . et cetera.

If the production is not a musical, the questions of what music (if any) is to be used in the production and who is responsible for dealing with the problem should be discussed now. This is separate from recordings and includes music between the acts by an orchestra in the pit, live music on- or offstage, or a musician to play offstage while the actor "fakes" playing. This problem is usually put into the hands of a competent musician, who, with the playwright, producer and director, selects the music and musicians. Sometimes the problem is left to the stage manager to settle. The general manager will advise the stage manager as to the disposition of the problem. Later the stage manager will discuss the matter with the designer when they plan cuing facilities and backstage arrangements.

DIRECTOR AND STAGE MANAGER

As soon as possible the stage manager consults with the director, and they discuss:

I. Rehearsal Schedule. The director will have his own method of directing. It is the job of the stage manager to adapt himself to it and help the director in every way. These methods vary greatly. Some directors plot a progress chart weeks in advance and manage to adhere to it. Others have an "Oh, we'll start by reading for a few days and then see what happens," method. The stage manager will be prepared to size up the situation immediately. One thing must not be forgotten. Time must be allotted for special rehearsals and performances for sound recordings or other "specials." With some directors this is no problem, but with a director who has no foreseeable plan, the stage manager must be an opportunist and seize time from the director to accomplish essential things. These latter directors are rare, fortunately. However, all people become absorbed in their work, and someone must have an eye on the clock to see that appointments are kept, that work gets done. The stage manager is the time keeper.

If a choreographer and a music department are involved, the scheduling problem becomes considerably more complex. In musical productions, it is customary for the dancers to begin rehearsals a week before the principals. If the production is heavy musically the singers will also begin rehearsals a week before the principals. The scheduling of this week is fairly simple. This is the time when the choreographer and choral director will block out the big numbers, although they will by no means have completed their work in this week. When the principals begin rehearsals the "book scenes" will have to be staged, work continued on the chorus numbers, soloists rehearsed, principals worked into the big musical numbers, principals' solo choreography worked out, costume and press appointments made and kept. All this work must proceed concurrently, with usually two or three rehearsals going on at the same time. The stage manager will try to get as much agreement among the director, choreographer and vocal director as possible regarding the general scheme of the rehearsal days. This will often require the tact and diplomacy of a Robespierre. The stage manager's ability to improvise will also be taxed to the fullest. The ideal rehearsal situation is to use everyone's time fully and profitably.

The stage manager will, after consultation with the director (and choreographer and musical director), work up a *Rehearsal Schedule.* This will contain, at the minimum, information as to the over-all times of rehearsal, lunch breaks, places of rehearsal and days off. This information will be given to the staff personnel as quickly as possible, so that their activities may be planned in relation to the rehearsals. For example, the costume designer must know the days off so that he will not plan costume fittings on that day.

II. Casting. The director will advise the stage manager on what parts have been cast and what is the method for future casting. Stars, featured players and some small-part actors may have been signed or decided upon before the stage manager has been hired, and an actors' file of some sort been established.

Some production offices will have a casting director on the staff. This person will be responsible for interviewing and auditioning actors and for the maintenance of files. The stage manager will familiarize himself with the casting director's methods and what specific problems present themselves for the production at hand. Suggestions and recommendations from the stage manager are often welcome. If the production office does not employ a casting director, much of that function will devolve upon the stage manager.

A. CAST LIST. A cast list for quick reference can be plotted like this:

CHARACTER	ACTOR	ALTERNATES	UNDERSTUDY
JOHN	Henry Henry (Enright)	1. John Jones (Broder) 2. Sam Smith (Broder) 3. Will Wilson (Morris)	Hanff Gonff
MARY	Eliza Licer (M.C.A.)	1. Mattie Matson (Enright) 2. Betty Boop (Liebling) 3. Catty Call (Morris)	Merribelle Dimples
ANN (Maid) Understudy	Merribelle Dimples	1. Susan Sloop 2. Hannah Humph	Lucy McGrew
JEEVES (Butler) Understudy	Hanff Gonff	1. Harry Heil 2. Bernie Bernard (Morris)	Dave Brown
POSTMAN (Understudy & Asst. SM)	Dave Brown	1. Jack Green	Jack Green
etc.	etc.	etc.	etc.

The names of alternates appear in order of preference. The names in parentheses are the actors' agents, if any.

B. ACTORS' FILE. The actors' file varies greatly in different producers' offices. Often a separate file is established for each new production. In any event the stage manager will be expected to keep this file up-to-date or furnish the material to do so. Usually the actor's card is filed alphabetically under the character name for which he is considered. The following information should be included on the card:

31

1. Actor's name, address, phone number.
2. Actor's agent, with notation whether or not agent is acting for him in this production.
3. Experience and special talents.
4. Part for which he is considered.
5. Possible other parts or understudy for which he is suited.
6. Date and comment on any reading and initials of those attending reading.

The actors' file includes a card for each actor considered for a part—not just interviewed but seriously considered—whether he has a reading or not. This is not the stupendous task that it appears to be at first glance, since by the time the stage manager comes on the scene, or the profession is aware that casting is being done, a large portion of the cast is set. This means that the stage manager, who may be assigned the responsibility of screening all prospects, has his work outlined for him in a definite pattern. The requirements of the handful of parts left to be filled will automatically exclude most applicants.

C. ACTORS' INTERVIEWS. Actors' Equity Association rules provide that two "Open Equity Calls" be set up for each production. At these calls Equity members will be seen and interviewed briefly. Briefly, because it is likely that hundreds of actors may appear during each of the four-hour calls. These calls are usually held in a theatre or rehearsal hall. A numbered sheet should be posted at the stage door so that actors who appear for the call will sign it in the order of arrival. They are called in that order and the interviewer need not waste his own time or the actor's if there is no part for the actor in the play being cast. Actors who may possess the qualifications for a role should be asked for a picture and resume and an appointment should be made for a reading or audition. This is a preliminary screening and is often in the hands of the stage manager. Notice should be given of these open calls to Equity at least a week in advance.

Chorus Equity requires singers' and dancers' auditions to be scheduled a week in advance also. The date must be cleared with Equity so that two shows do not have auditions on the same day. An Equity representative will be on hand for the chorus calls and will distribute numbered cards for the performers to fill out. The choreographer will be in charge of the dancers' auditions and the composer or choral director in charge of the singers'.

Because of the large number of actors who show up for these calls, some theatre personnel have the tendency to think of them as "cattle calls." They are not! While a great many actors must be seen in a limited time, it must never be forgotten that they are artists and that the job at hand is to fill roles in a play. If four hundred actors are seen and only *one* finds his way into the cast of the play, the time has not been wasted for it is possible that this particular actor could have been found in no other way.

Three basic tests should be applied to the applicant for an acting job:

1. External or physical qualifications
2. The applicant's technique
3. The caliber of the applicant's innate ability

These are not in the order of importance, but in the order of obviousness.

Certain requirements, such as sex, age or a physical characteristic, cannot be circumvented. The prospect's experience and ability will not help him if he cannot fill these obvious requirements.

The ideal actor would be the individual whose body and mind are under such perfect control that he could call on any one of a complete range of attributes, or any combination of them, in order to portray any characterization. There is no need to enter into a discussion of the reasons some actors never achieve this control. Suffice it to say that they do not. They limit their range to those attributes which are similar to their outstanding and most-cultivated personal traits. Consequently the parts they play are restricted in scope. In general terms, they "play their personalities," or they are "types."

The experienced interviewer is immediately aware of the applicant's outstanding traits, and, if these traits coincide with the attributes necessary for a particular characterization, there has been a fortunate meeting. However, unless the interviewer is thoroughly familiar with the applicant's work, he will not know whether or not these apparent traits are the only ones in the applicant's range. This must be determined before an applicant is rejected, or valuable acting material may be overlooked. A brief review of the parts the actor has played may indicate his acting range. However, unless the interviewer has knowledge of the caliber of the companies with which the actor performed, and also has an exhaustive familiarity with the plays, a review of the actor's career is of little help.

Sometimes a more satisfactory and accurate examination of the prospect may be made by having him give a reading from the manuscript.

If the interviewer feels that the prospect is capable of a characterization, he should refer the prospect to the producer and the director. If he is certain that the prospect cannot do the job, he should tell him so immediately.

It is at this stage of casting that the difference between adequate casting and exceptional casting is determined. Casting that stops with the use of the obvious personality may be adequate, but it is rarely exceptional. Casting that digs out latent, unknown or unused ability, may achieve exceptional results.

There have been many terms used in evaluating an actor's caliber. Some of them have been graphic. An actor of fine caliber "has it," or has "oomph," or "sends one." If his caliber is poor, he "leaves you cold." The use of these words is colorful, but too frequently they are adopted by inexperienced persons and, through misuse, lose their color and meaning. The conscientious casting interviewer will want more than general knowledge of the quality that determines caliber in an actor. Also he will want a yardstick by which he can measure his own ability as a judge. The psychologists have a word that helps. The word is empathy.

A thing (a voice, a color, any "thing") can induce an emotion. Empathy is the imaginative process that endows the thing with the emotion the thing has induced in the receiver. For example, a marble statue may induce in an observer sensations of coolness, serenity and happiness. If the observer, by imagination projection, endows the statue

34

with these qualities, the statue itself (to the observer) becomes cool, serene and happy. This imaginative process is empathy.

All individuals have the power or quality that generates this imaginative process in an observer. Some have the power to a large degree and consequently can reach and influence a large number of receivers. Others have the quality to a lesser degree. This power, this quality, is frequently called empathic appeal. Those who have empathic appeal in large quantities can be found everywhere. They may be a butcher, baker, or housewife—they do not have to be in some branch of what is called entertainment. Quite often they do not consciously recognize that they have such appeal, or that they have put in motion the empathic process. However, to be an actor, one *must* have empathic appeal to a large degree, and one must be conscious of it and capable of utilizing it to generate the proper stimuli.

In the theatre, empathy, or the empathic process, has two important partners, the actor and the receiver, without whom there can be no process. The actor, with his empathic appeal, generates the stimulus. The receiver accepts the stimulus in the form of emotions, and imaginatively projects them back into the actor and endows the actor with them. Consequently the caliber of both actor and receiver determines the completeness and effectiveness of the empathic process. An actor with limited empathic appeal will generate correspondingly fewer and less powerful stimuli than an actor with great appeal. Also, an actor with a great appeal may be ineffective to a poorly-conditioned receiver. As a casting interviewer is a receiver, he must be prepared to recognize empathic appeal caliber. By looking deeply into his own conditioning, he makes certain that he is prepared.

It can be seen that any person who approaches the problems of casting a play should do so with considerable forethought and caution. A stage manager, entrusted with the job of interviewing actors, will need infinite patience, ingenuity, imagination, experience, theatre background and personal discipline. He must constantly examine and evaluate his own, as well as the public's, receptivity to empathic appeal. And he must know how to recognize this appeal in actors who have not as yet learned to control it and present it with facility.

The actual mechanics of the interview are simple, if the interviewer is prepared. The only proper treatment of an applicant is honesty. Those that are obviously not suited for a part should be told so immediately. Most actors appreciate such frankness. A file card need not be made for these rejects, but a record of the interview is valuable. Those actors who fall within the proper categories should be interviewed briefly and to the point: get name, address, agent, experience, and make a few identifying notes. Then tell them the truth, which is usually: their names are being taken for reference only; the producer is considering others; they may or may not be given an interview or reading with the director and producer; in the meantime they should not turn down any opportunity for other employment; the failure to get a part in this play does not militate against getting a part in a future production.

At first glance this may appear to be a form of "run-around." It is not. In addition to each actor settled upon for a part, the producer will want at least three alternates available. Thus, at least four possible applicants are needed. Common sense tells the stage manager that he cannot score perfectly each time with his first four choices. He must have a larger group from which the producer can make a selection. If out of fifteen to twenty "possibles" four finalists can be selected, the score is above average. The actor should understand that he is on a "possible" list and that his chance for the part is—and this is a highly optimistic figure—no better than one in twenty. When the actor knows this, he will understand that he is not "getting a run-around."

Once in a while an actor especially right for a part will come along. Try to have the producer and the director furnish a schedule of times when they are available to see applicants, so that the applicant may be given a definite appointment then and there. Take more copious notes on this actor, and add them to his file card. The cards of the applicants can be given to the producer and the director before they hold the interviews. This helps the interviewer prepare for a more thorough and satisfactory interview.

D. AUDITIONS AND READINGS. The terms *reading* and *audition* are used by many people interchangeably. The purist will use *reading* to indicate a test of the actor by means of the dialogue. *Audition* will indicate something physical, such as an ability to dance, sing, play the trombone or stand on one's head. Very often the test of the actor will include elements of both readings and auditions. This handbook uses the term *reading* most of the time, but the reader may substitute audition if he wishes, as the methods of conducting each are fundamentally the same.

Auditions or readings should be reduced to a minimum when possible. As noted before, in the average cast many of the parts will have been filled before the stage manager is hired. This leaves only a few readings necessary, but even those must be kept to a minimum and handled with dispatch. In most cases the producer and the director will have a preferred or established system for handling these readings, and will outline it to the stage manager. Sometimes they will rely on the stage manager to devise a system. In any event it will devolve on the stage manager to organize the details and make the system function.

The stage manager should be acquainted with an Equity rule concerning readings: "Principals . . . shall not be called in groups, unless necessary for physical screening and/or voice blending . . . ." This means that the actor will generally read only with the stage manager or his assistant. Acting skill among stage managers varies, of course. However, the stage manager should learn to read well enough so that the actor gets at least a sense of playing a scene, not of reciting a lot of words. This does not mean developing "heavy" characterizations or changing one's voice drastically to suit the character. It does mean saying the lines with as much of the intention behind them as possible, and listening and playing "with" an actor. It is also wise to stand (if the readings are held on a stage) slightly downstage of the actor. It is, after all, the actor's reading and the producer and director want to get a look at *his* face. Presumably they will see quite enough of the stage manager's face in the weeks to follow.

Readings will necessarily include the playwright, the producer and the director, since their approval must be obtained for all casting. Others included may be the production's star, the stage managers, the actor's agent and the general manager. It is best to keep the number of

37

participants small. Some readings are held in the producer's office or apartment, where a relaxed and cozy atmosphere presumably exists. These *in camera* readings usually include only the playwright, producer, director and prospect. Other readings are quite formal and are held on a stage. Still others take place in a noisy corridor! Wherever held, the following preparations should be made:

1. The actor and his agent should be notified well in advance to prepare for the reading. This includes an opportunity for the actor to familiarize himself with the scene to be read.
2. The scenes to be read by each character should be decided beforehand, and sufficient copies of the manuscript or special copies of the scene should be on hand.
3. Specially edited copies of a scene are useful, because emphasis may be placed on the lines the prospect will read. Intervening lines by other characters may be shortened or eliminated. Thus a flow or continuity may be given the prospect's dialogue that isn't there in the complete manuscript. These scenes are prepared after permission is received from the playwright and the director.
4. A typed schedule of appointments should be on hand for all. This schedule should include:
   a. Date and time.
   b. Actor's name, agent, part for which he is considered.
   c. Space for notes and comment.

As soon as possible after the reading a decision should be made and reported to the actor or his agent. This reporting often is left to the stage manager and takes one of three forms:

a. Yes—the actor is hired.
b. No—the actor is not to be hired.
c. Perhaps—the actor is being considered along with several others, and a decision will be reached by next Tuesday.

A yes or no report should be given whenever possible. Stalling an actor or keeping him on tenterhooks can be very upsetting as well as financially disastrous, if he turns down other employment because of indecision. The stage manager should keep a record of actors being kept in abeyance and should try to get decisions about them made as soon as possible. After a reading, a note of its outcome should be made on the actor's file card.

To repeat, the number and length of readings should be kept small. Readings and auditions are very fatiguing for the listeners, and a tired judge is unfair to the actor and to the production.

E. UNDERSTUDIES. The producer, director, and playwright select the understudies. However, as the understudy setup may be complicated, the services of the general manager and stage manager are recruited. Also, the general manager handles the actors' contracts and must include in them the exact parts an actor is to understudy, and the salary he receives if he should play a part.

The following understudy situation should be avoided. The letters represent the actors in the company and the understudies who cover them:

A, B, C, D, E, F, G, H, J, X, Y, Z, Asst. Stg. Mgr.

A)
C)   Covered by E

B)
D)   Covered by G
F)

E)
G)   Covered by H

H)
J)   Covered by X

X)
Y)   Covered by Asst. Stg. Mgr.
Z)

If Actor C cannot perform he is replaced by Actor E and a chain of replacements follows ending with an acting company in this sequence (replacements in quotes):

A, B, "E," D, "H," F, G, "X," J, "Asst. Stg. Mgr.," Y, Z.
Four replacements necessary to adjust for one absence!
The following method of understudying is more satisfactory:

A) B) D) E)	Covered by X
C) F) G)	Covered by Y
X) Y) Z)	Covered by Asst. Stg. Mgr.

No matter which one actor is missing now, no more than two understudies will be used.

If more than one actor is absent, complications arise and lead to an elaboration often utilized. This is sometimes called "double-cover" and works like this: (Note that the stage manager is used. This is permitted by Equity on an "emergency" basis and for one or two performances only. If the actor's absences are to be longer, a new actor or understudy must be hired.)

		1st Cover	2nd Cover
A) B) D) E)	Covered by	X	Z
C) F) G) H) J)	Covered by	Y	Asst. Stg. Mgr.

40

		1st Cover	2nd Cover
X)			
Y)	Covered by	Asst. Stg Mgr.	Stage Manager
Z)			

With this type of understudy schedule it is seen that, when Actors B and D are absent, the parts are covered by Z and X, and the company appears as follows:

A, "X," "Z," E, C, F, G, H, J, "Asst. Stg. Mgr.," Y, "Stg. Mgr."
Not ideal, to be sure, but far better than losing a performance.

Very often a situation occurs in which no member of a company or the assistant stage manager is suitable as understudy for a part; e.g., in a company composed of middle-aged characters and a child, no member of the company can understudy the child. In this case another child will be hired. This nonpart-holding, nonappearing understudy is known as a "walking understudy."

The system of understudying for a particular production may involve a combination of several methods. It can be seen that establishing the system will take careful planning. Whatever plan is decided upon, it is essential that the understudies be hired at the same time as the actors, for they must attend all rehearsals. They receive the benefit of the director's work with the regular actors, are available to stand in during rehearsals, and are prepared to go on at dress rehearsals or openings. It is the duty of the stage manager to see that they are prepared.

Most producers look upon understudies as a form of insurance not unlike the more obvious fire and theft insurance, and are willing to pay weekly "premiums" for this insurance in the form of small additions to an actor's salary. This is arranged by the general manager at the time the actors' contracts are signed. The stage manager cannot expect the actor to assume more understudy work than he has contracted for.

In general, the use of understudies is an emergency measure, and most managements have a sensible attitude toward their use. The tradition that the show must go on is strong, but no show must go on using an actor if that actor will endanger his health. Managements will

41

prefer that an actor lose several performances and thus prevent serious illness rather than continue to perform and eventually lose weeks of performance. Also, the chance of infecting the other members of the company cannot be ignored.

With the above in mind, no actor should arrive at the theatre too sick to perform. If he arrives at the theatre at all, the management has the right to presume he is capable of going on. Should the actor find himself ill during the day, he should advise the management. This will give the stage manager, the understudy and the other actors a chance to prepare for the sick actor's absence. And so, in most cases, discussions in this handbook concern themselves with absences and the use of understudies that arise from sudden illness or accident.

DESIGNER AND STAGE MANAGER

I. First Conference. In the early prerehearsal days the stage manager should arrange a meeting with the scene designer. As his most frequent contacts will be with the designer's assistants, he should meet them also as soon as possible. This will be a get-acquainted meeting primarily, but the following should be accomplished:

    a. Discuss the production schedule thoroughly. Has enough time been allotted for take-in and set-up? For lighting?

    b. Get a ground plan of each set. Ground plans are usually made in ½-inch scale. If it is possible, the stage manager should ask the designer to provide him with a set of ¼-inch scale drawings. (This is usually done quite simply by the blueprint maker.) The ¼-inch scale drawings will be easier to handle in rehearsal for reference and will fit (folded once) into the prompt script.

    c. Study and thoroughly understand each set, using the scale models for study. Before and during rehearsals questions such as, "Is there room on this wall for a mirror?" "Which way does this door swing?" will be asked. The stage manager must have the answers ready.

    d. Turn over a copy of the preliminary plots to the designer. He undoubtedly will have more elaborate plots of his own, but a cross-check is essential. Discuss the lighting especially.

e. Discuss the position of the prompt desk in relation to the scenery. This will entail a discussion of cuing facilities and should be as thorough as possible.

f. Discuss the building and placement of quick-change rooms in the wings, and other specials.

g. Arrange with the designer a time for a daily exchange of information. It should be understood that one of the functions of the designer is the design and procurement of properties. As the list of properties, as well as other elements of the production, will undergo change and elaboration during the rehearsal period, it is essential that the designer be apprised of changes promptly. He cannot be in attendance at all rehearsals. To accomplish this there should be a daily meeting, in person or over the phone, between the designer or his assistants and the stage manager. In this handbook this meeting is called an *information exchange.*

In his position as liaison staff member, the stage manager must be prepared to do a certain amount of shopping or selection of properties and other production elements. He is often the only staff member, other than the director, who has exact knowledge of what is needed. Normally this information can be conveyed to the designer during the information exchange, but, to save valuable time, the stage manager may help make the actual selection. In these instances, the stage manager works in conjunction with the designer. The designer passes on the element's appropriateness in matters of taste, the stage manager in matters of practicability.

h. Determine what equipment the designer will require while lighting the show, e.g., intercom set.

i. Enlist the designer's help in obtaining special rehearsal props or scenic elements to be used for rehearsal. (This will have been previously discussed with the director.)

II. Lighting Conference. The production electrician is selected as soon as possible by the general manager, the designer and sometimes the stage manager. The electrician will assist the designer to select, prepare and adapt the lighting equipment, while working in the shop which will furnish the equipment. He may help manufacture special effects and other equipment.

The designer, the stage manager and the electrician should have a conference at which the designer will outline his plan for the lighting of the production. This is discussed thoroughly. This very essential meeting eliminates or forestalls many future problems. The stage manager will furnish a cuing layout at this conference, especially any light-cue system that the electrician will furnish or prepare.

PRESS AGENT AND STAGE MANAGER

The press agent will enlist the services of the stage manager in having the actors fill out publicity information blanks, making and keeping appointments, etc. The press agent is not passing the buck in this matter. On the contrary, the stage manager should insist on handling these things, because by doing so he can prevent interrupting rehearsals and wasting valuable time. The stage manager does not initiate publicity appointments and the like, but he should screen and co-ordinate them.

COMPANY MANAGER AND STAGE MANAGER

The company manager is really an assistant general manager, and many of the stage manager's contacts with him will be the same as those with the general manager. However, they will work closely on such matters as having the actors fill out tax-withholding blanks, social security blanks, etc., in order not to waste rehearsal time.

COSTUME DESIGNER AND STAGE MANAGER

The stage manager will arrange times with the costume designer for the measurement of actors. (Equity permits one two-hour measurement call for each actor before rehearsals begin). The costume designer will know the schedules of the costume shop and may wish to be present at the measurement so that he can get an idea of the actors' coloring and other requirements.

44

It must not be construed from the foregoing that the conferences listed comprise all the conferences the stage manager will attend. These are merely the ones he must initiate himself. He should attend all conferences, because in his role as the liaison staff member he must know practically all details of the production if he is to accomplish his liaison work intelligently.

THE STAR AND STAGE MANAGER

The stage manager usually meets the star many days before rehearsals start. He should be aware of the traditions governing his and other personnel's treatment of the star. Courtesy is as necessary in the theatre as anywhere else. Unfortunately a newcomer may misinterpret these courtesies for sycophancy in the giver and for arrogance in the receiver.

The recruit in the army soon learns that military courtesy, demanding that he stand at attention when being addressed by a superior, is more than "respect for rank." It is also an indication that the soldier is conscious of the things inherent in the word "attention": readiness, alertness, industry and an awareness that time cannot be wasted. In a like manner the courtesies given in the theatre to the star, and in turn accepted and expected by him, are in actuality a form of insurance against wasting time and energy.

In the limited rehearsal period, the star has much more to accomplish than the other members of the company. The star will have more dialogue to learn, more costumes to fit, more appointments to meet, will spend more time onstage. It is a matter of simple economy that this individual must be given every aid to accomplish a maximum of work with a minimum of effort, so that strength may be preserved and health safeguarded. If approached with this understanding in mind, it will be seen that "privileges of the star" are not added niceties or the trappings of rank but very important adjuncts to the production.

When schedules are being made or appointments decided, it is customary to consult the star in advance. Help in obtaining transportation to and from rehearsals, seclusion for study when not needed at rehearsal, a close watch for fatigue, promptness on everyone's part, tailoring rehearsal lights, heat, and such things to best fit the star's well-being are among the many courtesies that may be extended.

If the star finds it necessary to demand courtesies, a close look into the root of the demand usually finds it is not a protest against an imaginary indignity of *lese-majeste* but a sincere disapproval of waste and bad management. The same roots often underlie "temperamental outbursts."

It will be the responsibility of the stage manager to see that traditional courtesies are extended to the star, the hardest-working member of the company. This may mean explaining the reasons behind these courtesies to inexperienced personnel, and, unfortunately, may mean *demanding* courtesy from thoughtless and inconsiderate persons.

Often unavoidable technical or other problems will arise which will seem to be time-wasting because they are not understood. The stage manager will seldom be too busy to explain to the star why work cannot procede smoothly.

THE COMPANY AND STAGE MANAGER

Every actor considers a production "my show." The show will be the center of his existence for weeks, months and, hopefully, years. If every actor is treated with the courtesy and respect to which his profession entitles him, he will in turn find it easy to maintain pride in his performance, his professionalism, his respect for his colleagues, and his work. The stage manager can "set the tone" by his unfailing courtesy to each member of the production.

PREPARATION FOR THE FIRST REHEARSAL

Check List:
1. Do the actors and understudies required for the first rehearsal (this may not be *all* actors) know the time and place of the first rehearsal?
2. Have all actors and understudies scripts?

3. Has Actors' Equity been advised of time and place of first rehearsal?
4. Has a list of all actors, including understudies and stage managers, been prepared and sent to the Equity representative?
5. Has the rehearsal hall been checked well in advance of the rehearsal for:
   a. size? .
   b. lights?
   c. heat?
   d. adequate tables, chairs, and ashtrays (enough for both setting the scene and the use of actors who are waiting)?
   e. smoking rules and facilities?
   f. drinking water?
   g. toilets?
   h. available phones? Has the office the numbers?
   i. an attendant at the rehearsal hall? Does he know about the rehearsal?
6. Are ground plans and models of all sets available?
7. Are there extra manuscripts immediately available?
8. Is there a supply of paper and pencils on hand?
9. Has a daily attendance chart been made to record the rehearsal hours of each actor, individually and in detail?
10. Do the producer, director, playwright, scenic and other designers and press agent know the time and place of the rehearsal?
11. Has the stage floor been marked with the ground plan?
12. Has the stage manager familiarized himself with Actors' Equity and other union rules concerning rehearsals?
13. Have the stage managers a pocketful of dimes for phone calls?
14. Is the prompt script prepared?

STAGE MANAGERS EQUIPMENT

Mention should be made of the equipment the stage manager will need. Over a period of years many stage managers accumulate a good deal of equipment which they find useful, particularly during tryouts and road tours, and it will be listed later. They use this equipment during rehearsals and New York runs because they have it, not because it is absolutely essential. There are things, however, the stage manager is expected to have:

1. A briefcase of some sort.
2. Dozens (literally) of sharpened pencils with erasers and some means of keeping them sharpened.
3. Scratch pads.
4. A clipboard—invaluable for note-taking and keeping plots, appointments, etc., handy.
5. A measure of some sort, preferably two: a 12" ruler and a 6' folding rule or 25' cloth tape.
6. Chalk.
7. A watch and possibly a stop watch. The stop watch should be of the "sports timer" variety which allows starting, stopping, and resuming without resetting. This permits the stage manager to keep accurate record of the playing time even when there are many interruptions (times-out). Early in rehearsals the stage manager will want to time certain scenes, particularly cover scenes for costume changes and the like, and will report his findings to the director.
8. A diary. This will be used for recording appointments, absences, running times of run-throughs. It should be referred to the first thing in the morning and brought up to date the last thing in the evening.

All the above, along with manuscripts and ground plans, can be carried in the briefcase and should be sufficient to get rehearsals started. Many stage managers find a typewriter indispensable. Others get along without one, using office machines when necessary. The stage manager's equipment, like the sidewalk pitchman's, should be easily assembled and portable.

PART TWO

Rehearsals, First Weeks

The rehearsal period is short and consequently a time of great activity and intense concentration. The stage manager must see that time is not wasted. If he has a well-planned daily schedule, he is at an advantage. This schedule will be flexible, in order to adjust to changes made by the producer and the director; but, as certain things must be accomplished each day, it is wise to have them clearly in mind.

DAILY PREPARATION

I. Before Going To Rehearsal. Contact the office for last-minute advice. As the office may not open until approximately the same time that rehearsals start, it is often impossible for the stage manager to go personally to the office, and so contact may be made by phone.

II. At Rehearsal Hall. Be at rehearsal early to:
1. Advise office of phone numbers. The hall may not have been used previously, and the office will want to know how to make contact during the rehearsals.
2. Check light, heat, etc.
3. Prepare stage for rehearsal, including:
   a. If using a marked ground cloth, is it in place? Are tapes or chalk marks for proper set?
   b. Is the proper furniture in place?
   c. Are necessary rehearsal props available?
4. Check in actors, using "attendance record chart." This chart must be kept accurately. From it will be determined the first day of rehearsal for each actor, end of probationary period for each actor, exact time of each rehearsal, and rehearsal salary due each actor. Make sure absences and latenesses are recorded in the diary.
5. Transfer manuscript changes that have been received after the last rehearsal into actors' scripts.

6. Assign appointments for costume fittings, publicity, etc. These can be on separate reminder slips to hand the actor.
7. If another rehearsal hall is to be used in the future, have arrangements been made to transfer the ground cloth, rehearsal props, and other necessities?
8. Make final check with the director before rehearsal starts:
   a. acquaint him with appointments. He will have approved them before they are set, but he should be reminded.
   b. remind him of the status of actors on probation.
   c. establish the time the noon (or meal) recess will occur. Also the reconvening time and when rehearsal will be over for the day.

THE REHEARSAL

As a part of the first rehearsal, but before rehearsing or reading starts, the stage manager, in the presence of a representative of Actors' Equity, will read Equity rules to the company. Thereafter the stage manager is required to see that the rules are posted at the rehearsal hall during all rehearsals.

It will be essential for the stage managers to divide their work. As the prompt script is a full-time job for the stage manager, the assistant stage managers take over most of the other stage managerial rehearsal duties.

I. Rehearsal Duties of Assistants. The stage manager departmentalizes the duties of his assistants. A division of work might be as follows:

Asst. A:
1. Actors:
   Check their attendance.
   Check their entrances and exits.
   Keep actors available. This does not mean "tying them to the stage," but no actor should leave the immediate vicinity without permission from the stage manager.
2. Properties:
   Arrange rehearsal furniture.
   Prepare rehearsal hand props.

50

Asst. B:
1. Costumes:
    Record costume plot changes.
    Co-ordinate appointments for fittings, etc.
2. Handle all appointments.
3. Handle publicity forms, tax forms, other paper work.

Together—the assistants will:
1. Answer all phone calls and take messages.
2. Maintain quiet and order.
    a. It cannot be overemphasized that rehearsal days are few with limited hours, and, consequently, a period of concentration requiring a minimum of waste. The director's method will dictate the conduct of the stage managers, and they must do everything they can to ease the director's burden. If the director has not made clear his wishes before rehearsals, alert stage managers will soon determine them.
    b. Movement or sound is distracting. Have actors not engaged in a scene wait as far offstage and downstage in the wings as possible, not upstage where they are in the director's line of vision. If actors enter from different sides of the stage, try to have them on the proper side before starting the scene, thus avoiding distracting crossings of the stage.
    c. The director usually prefers to be alone in the auditorium. Keep actors and all others out.
    d. Shut all doors leading to the rehearsal area.
    e. Advise doorman of rehearsal hours and names of the cast. He can be very useful in turning away unwanted visitors.
    f. Muffle telephone bells if necessary.
    g. Rehearsal lights are notoriously bad. Endeavor to eliminate glare, and restrict bright lighting to the acting area.
    h. Actors will adjust themselves to a routine and to an established personnel. Keep visitors away unless you can announce to all that they are expected. Make sure that the cast meets new actors joining the company.

51

3. Protect rehearsal hall property. Rehearsals are often held in a theatre where there is a show in residence. All properties, scenery, costumes, of the incumbent must be left alone. Nothing may be used at any time for any purpose unless permission is received from the resident show's producer. Especial care must be taken during wet weather. Umbrellas, galoshes, wet clothing, can be very destructive. *Smoking rules must be enforced!*

II. Stage Manager's Duties. The stage manager prefers to handle the prompt script and related matters himself. He will watch the direction carefully, recording in the script all stage business, dialogue changes, and pertinent directions given. He will make notes on all props, costumes, lights, sound, etc., that are "created" or discussed during the rehearsal.

The stage manager usually works at a table placed near the footlights at one side of the stage beside the proscenium arch, where he can have an unobstructed view of the stage and the director in the auditorium. He chooses the side where his prompt desk will ultimately be when the scenery is used. Thus the actors may get accustomed to finding him in the same place.

A. TAKING NOTES. A convenient method of recording notes is to keep a sheet of paper handy on which columns with the following headings have been ruled:

Director	Mgr.	Designer	Costumes	Lights	Props	Misc.

Should any staff member appear at the rehearsal, a quick glance will suffice to find out if there are notes for him.

B. RECORDING STAGE DIRECTIONS. The markings, abbreviations, and symbols used in a prompt script to record action, emotion, tempo, and other elements are a type of shorthand and vary from stage manager to stage manager. There are certain traditional symbols that all

52

theater people use. Standard stage-area abbreviations are indicated on the following chart. U. means Upstage, D. is Downstage, R. is Rightstage, L. is Leftstage, and C. is Centerstage. Thus U.R. is Upstage Rightstage, or more commonly, Up Right. D.L.C. is Down Left Center.

U.R.	U.R.C.	U.C.	U.L.C.	U.L.
R.	R.C.	C.	L.C.	L.
D.R.	D.R.C.	D.C.	D.L.C.	D.L.

The above fifteen stage-area abbreviations normally suffice for the actors' onstage positions. Furniture or parts of the scenery are helpful locators. For example: "at window," "R. of table," "in doorway," or "on 3rd step" locate an actor immediately.

The letter X is frequently used to indicate a stage movement or cross. "X D.R." means "Cross to Down Right area." Small diagrams with arrows help clarify complicated movements.

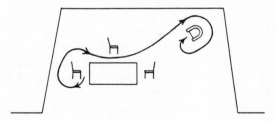

Complicated seating or other arrangements may be diagrammed. Initials signify characters' names.

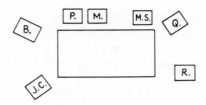

Recording characterization, emotion, and tempo is more difficult. The stage manager will want an accurate record of these elements for two reasons. First, the producer expects to find them in the prompt script, and second, they are invaluable as references when checking performances months later. The stage manager does not indulge in flights of description when recording. Succinctness is essential. By attending closely to all directions, all discussions of characterization, emotion, and meaning, the stage manager can spot several words or a short phrase that will sum up the complete discussion. These are the words he records. With a little practice and experience he will find that he will choose the words that serve as a cue to remind him of the complete direction or discussion. He records characterization, interpretation, and emotion in this manner.

Recording tempo imposes still another problem. Some stage managers find the signs used in written music valuable for this purpose. Crescendo and diminuendo signs may indicate tempo and volume changes; rest signs of different types may indicate pauses of various lengths. Another method of indicating pauses is to insert a vertical line between words where the pause occurs. Additional parallel vertical lines between the words may be added for longer pauses. Each line can indicate a pause of one "count," or approximately one second. Underscoring, bracketing, dashes, and so on may also be used.

Various characteristics of speech, such as inflection, dialect, and pronounciation, may be recorded by using accent marks, underscoring, dashes, and phonetic symbols.

Those stage managers familiar with shorthand (Gregg, Pitman, or Speedwriting) often use shorthand characters for quick recording. Incidentally, a knowledge of shorthand will be useful to the stage manager at all times. Some words and marks used in proofreading—

delete, stet, Λ (insert), tr or ~ (transpose), etc.—are valuable. All methods, all abbreviations and symbols, well-known or personal, must be transcribed by the stage manager into plain, simple language at the first opportunity.

C. ANSWERING QUESTIONS. Among the duties the stage manager is most frequently called on to perform is answering questions. As preparing and holding the prompt script will require his undivided attention most of the time, the stage manager should train actors and other backstage personnel not to disturb him when he is working. Most questions can be answered by the assistant stage managers, if the stage manager has shared his knowledge of production details with them. Therefore, questions should be addressed to the assistants first. If it is absolutely necessary to disturb the stage manager, personnel can be trained to approach the stage manager, get his attention without speaking to him, and wait until the stage manager may divide his attention at a time when doing so will not interfere with his job. Establishing this habit early in rehearsals is very valuable, as it will be essential procedure during technical or dress rehearsals and performances.

D. PROMPTING. There is no hard and fast rule governing when to and when not to prompt. Usually prompting will not start during the first week of rehearsal. During that week both the stage manager and the actor will be occupied marking stage business in their scripts. After business is set and lines learned, prompting starts.

Prompting should be the responsibility of one and the same stage manager throughout rehearsals and opening performances. The actors will become accustomed to the prompter's position, his face, and his voice. The stage manager will discover the actor's memorizing habits, his pauses, his character development, and particular passages in his dialogue he is having difficulty remembering. This rapport between actor and prompter will more often be the clue to when to prompt than any other one thing. It also will be the clue to when *not* to prompt, which is just as important.

Actors' memory patterns or habits vary but generally require one of two types of dialogue promptings. The first is the "key word" or "action word" or "meaning" prompt. The second is the "complete phrase" or "first word" type. These may be illustrated with the following line: "In due time surrender may be expected." Using the first typ:, the prompter would say, "Surrender." Using the second, "In due time surrender . . ." However, in this line, "Surrender may be expected in due time," the word "surrender" should serve both types. The stage manager must be alert to the individual actor's idiosyncrasies.

When prompting first starts, the prompter should use a clear, strong, normal voice. The actor wants help, not subtleties. As rehearsals progress, the volume may be decreased until the prompter can be heard only on the stage. Whispered prompts are not good. They often can be heard in all parts of the auditorium, whereas a low-volume, normal tone will not. During the final rehearsals the prompter tries to sustain the emotional content of the scene when prompting. This may sound rather fanciful, but it is not. A strident prompt can destroy the mood of a quiet scene, and a drawled prompt can ruin a quick tempo.

Some directors insist that the prompter stop the actor and correct him when he makes a mistake, no matter how small. Certain actors dislike this method. Other directors want prompting done only when the actor has "dried up" completely, and will reserve corrections until the end of the scene. There are those actors who dislike this method. It is a director's problem to decide which type of prompting the individual actor will receive. The stage manager should have this problem settled early in the rehearsal schedule, so that rehearsals will be smooth-running. If corrections are withheld until the end of the scene, the stage manager must record errors for future reference. One method of recording errors is to make light pencil check marks in the manuscript margin and underline the error in the dialogue. These marks can be erased easily after the error is corrected. Often the error is a recurrent one, and then the marks may be left in the script as a signpost that there may be "prompting ahead."

Most stage managers use this technique while "following the script." They watch the actor most of the time, making quick glances at the script to keep succeeding dialogue clearly in mind. A pencil may be used by placing its point on the line *following* the line being delivered by the actor. When glancing at the script the prompter's eye immediate-

56

ly goes to the correct place in the manuscript, he freshens his mind with succeeding dialogue, advances his pencil another line, and then glances back at the actor. Thus he is always "ahead" of the actor.

Some prompters glue their eyes to the manuscript and prompt by ear only. This has disadvantages. During rehearsals the actor is experimenting. If he interrupts his dialogue, he may be testing the length of a pause for emotional or action reasons. Should the prompter not be watching, he will not realize that the actor is in full control, but will guess that he is "up" and consequently may throw an unwanted and highly disconcerting prompt. Moreover, the only way the stage manager can be in rapport with the actor, can find out what he does at all times, is by looking at him!

Except for the learning period of rehearsals, prompting should be considered an emergency measure, and actors should not use the prompter as a crutch to bolster indifferent memories. However, when a prompt is needed it must be given quickly and clearly. The mental block that creates the need for a prompt must be penetrated. Whatever the cause of the lapse of memory may be, the actor must be set back on the right track before panic sets in.

In the final analysis the best answer to prompting is to insist that the actor learn his dialogue quickly and accurately!

E. ACTING AS ASSISTANT DIRECTOR. The stage manager does not train or direct the actors without explicit permission from the director. Any attempt on his part to do so will be considered an encroachment on the director's province and will not be tolerated. Directing chores turned over to the stage manager will be specific. Such things as blocking out the movements of a crowd of extras and assigning individual lines to members of the crowd fall into this category. If an actor approaches the stage manager with problems of interpretation and characterization, he must be referred to the director.

There are some aspects that come under the general heading of direction that the stage manager does and will be expected to handle. These concern themselves with technical details of the production. If, during the rehearsal, the actor is pantomiming the opening of a window and indicates he thinks it is a sash-type window, when in reality it is a casement window, the stage manager should correct this error. It is not necessary to stop rehearsals to do this, if the mistake concerns this actor only. It may be corrected before or after rehearsal or during a rest period. However, if the error concerns later business, plotting, or dialogue, the attention of the director should be called to the error. These errors should be spotted early in the rehearsal period and corrected immediately. If the actor is permitted to continue in error, he will establish habits that will be upsetting when he finds himself in the scenery.

Unanticipated occasions arise when the director may be late to a rehearsal. The stage manager should take over the running of the rehearsal and prevent loss of rehearsal time. If the director has not made provisions for such emergency absences, the stage manager must use his own judgment. Reviewing work done at previous rehearsals is the general practice. Line rehearsals or walking rehearsals of scenes that have been broken in previously will help the actor set his part. Introducing new material or going on to scenes as yet unrehearsed should not be considered. That is the director's job. Any activity—arranging appointments, discussion of technical matters, checking manuscripts, and so on—that eliminates wasting valuable time should be taken up on these occasions.

In the case of a director who is not a good planner, the stage manager will find himself becoming more and more the assistant director. When and how he assists will depend on many things, but usually such matters as what to rehearse the next day, when to rehearse, time of appointments, and such "technical" functions will fall into the category of duties the stage manager may assume. The stage manager will avoid such things as actor's characterizations, line readings, and other "creative" parts of the director's job unless his assistance is specifically requested. Good common sense and plenty of tact should see a stage manager through rehearsals conducted in this manner.

There are directors who, although quite capable of doing their own planning, will expect the stage manager to prepare rehearsal schedules and such matters for them. The stage manager will be alert to what the director may require from him.

THE NOON (OR MEAL) RECESS

Check:
1. Do all personnel know the time and place to reconvene? This may be a place other than the location of the morning rehearsal.
2. Phone office to advise that morning rehearsal is over and where and when reconvening.
3. Advise director of status of actors on probation.
4. Hold Information Exchange. (See page 43.) This is not an ideal time as the recess is usually only an hour and a half, but some days it is the only available time.

BEFORE DISMISSAL OF ACTORS AT END OF REHEARSAL DAY

Check:
1. Status of actors on probation.
2. Does everyone know the time and place of the next rehearsal? This may mean holding the actors until a conference between the director, star, and stage manager is held.
3. Can any appointments be given out?
4. Have all actors received changes in dialogue?
5. Contact office for late advices for actors.
6. Has Equity Deputy been elected?
7. Have there been any changes of address?
8. Remind actors to take home their scripts and study them.
9. Pick up publicity blanks, tax blanks, etc.
10. Try to gather in some of the pencils that have been borrowed!

AFTER REHEARSAL

I. Staff Conference. Some producers have a staff conference after the day's rehearsing is over. The stage manager attends this conference and delegates the following duties to his assistants:
1. Supervise transfer of ground cloth, rehearsal props, etc. to the new rehearsal hall; or, if no change is being made, see that they

are safely stored. See that no personal or company property is left behind.

2. Hold Information Exchange with designers or their assistants. At the conference the stage manager will help arrange appointments and future schedules and will take notes pertinent to his department. He will pass on these notes to his assistants later.

II. Stage Managers' Daily Meeting. If the producer does not have regular and formal staff meetings, the stage manager's first duty is to check with the office for advice. The producer may not have been able to attend rehearsals and will want a progress report. This is the time to discuss with the producer or business manager all problems that have arisen during the day that the stage manager cannot settle.

When immediate matters (staff conference, disposal of ground cloth, etc.) are settled, the stage manager and his assistants will gather together for their daily meeting, or Clearing House. The purpose of this meeting is to tie in all the loose ends in the day's business, to exchange ideas, and to plan future activity.

This stage managers' meeting often is held in the producer's office, where stationery, typewriters, and other office facilities, especially telephones, are available. If the office has a PBX switchboard, a half-hour's instruction in its operation from the office switchboard operator will be invaluable to the stage manager, since this meeting normally is held after regular office hours. The business manager will make arrangements for these meetings, furnishing keys to the office and advising the office building employees that the stage managers are bona fide members of his staff and may be admitted to the building at irregular hours. At this meeting the following should be accomplished:

A. ROUTINE.

1. Discuss notes taken at staff conference.
2. Make a list of the following day's appointments in triplicate, one each for the producer, director, and stage managers, and arrange transportation if necessary. Separate appointment slips should be made for each actor, showing type of appointment, date and time, address, best means of transportation.
3. Bring actors' file up-to-date.

4. Clear up status of actors in abeyance.
5. Bring expense account up-to-date.
6. Bring address list up-to-date
7. Hold Information Exchange with designer (if not already held).
8. Bring prompt script up-to-date. Where applicable, notes should be transferred into the technical plots.

Many of the stage manager's rehearsal notes will be written hastily. Some stage directions may be a series of arrows; actors' stage positions may be shown by a small diagram, e.g., a group around a table. These should be clarified and inserted into the manuscript while they are in mind. It should be remembered that the final manuscript will be reproduced on a standard typewriter.

In revising the manuscript, page numbers should be retained until all active manuscripts, those used by actors and staff members, can be renumbered simultaneously. Completely renumbering the prompt script pages daily is an unnecessary chore and makes reference between manuscripts held by different staff members difficult. Added pages can bear the preceding page number plus an identifying *"a," "b," "c,"* etc. If the production secretary is hired to keep the manuscript freshly typed, his services should be used at this time. The secretary can relieve the stage manager of much typing, and the stage manager can furnish the secretary information about stage directions.

Many stage managers have a practice of not "cleaning up" the prompt script after a certain point in the rehearsal period. This practice has sound foundations and will be discussed later in Part Three, Section Two. However, during these early rehearsals the manuscript must be kept fresh.

A manuscript is not up-to-date unless a theater-wise person, unfamiliar with the production, can read it and understand it at sight.

B. TRAINING ASSISTANTS. This meeting can be a valuable opportunity for the stage manager to train his assistants. The stage manager's sights are set on the performance of the play. He has been planning and revising performance pattern constantly. He will share his plans with his assistants and accept suggestions from them. One of the stage manager's most necessary qualities is an ability to anticipate. Experience, of course, is the greatest help a stage manager may have in anticipating. Yet anticipation is also a frame of mind, a point of view, usually a questioning one. This handbook's primary purpose is to help the inexperienced anticipate his problems. The experienced stage manager will help his assistants, particularly with problems peculiar to a particular production.

1. Division of Duties. Just as rehearsal duties are departmentalized, performance duties, too, will be split up among the stage managers. It is wise to carry over rehearsal duties to the performance. The assistant in charge of checking actors at rehearsal will be in charge of checking them at performances. The assistant in charge of rehearsal props should be in charge of performance props.

Most stage managers go through the play line by line, move by move, and plan each stage manager's action, physical and mental. They do this when all assistants are in attendance, as each must be familiar with the other's duties. It will be decided how each cue is accomplished, how each element of the production is checked, and who will supervise the checking—be the double-check. They will study and revise the performance pattern, ironing out difficulties and conflicts. No element is too small or unimportant or obvious not to be considered and discussed. These discussions of the performance pattern should be a free exchange of ideas and suggestions between the stage managers.

2. Emergencies. a) Anticipation and the Performance Pattern. The stage manager should develop the habit of thinking out loud when with his assistants, and should encourage them to do the same. Continual asking of the question "What do I do if . . . ?" and finding the answer, will anticipate most emergencies, and anticipation prevents apprehension. The more completely the stage managers foresee emergencies, and have mental drills of their procedure for emergencies, the less apprehensive they will be about them. The question "What do I do if ... ?" ceases to be formidable, if the stage managers have trained themselves by correct thinking patterns to act quickly and properly in emergencies.

The reader should not get the impression that the stage manager goes about in a state bordering on panic. He does not, or he should not. Nevertheless, things will go wrong. The best defense against errors is a strong performance pattern.

Many anecdotes are told about backstage accidents or emergencies. An actor fainted or the scenery collapsed, but, because of quick action, the "audience never knew." Most of these stories are true. The credit given individuals for covering the error is well placed. But it will be found that, because of anticipation and thorough training of all departments, the play had a good performance pattern, and that, basically, the pattern was the real hero.

School children have a performance pattern in their fire drills. Soldiers learn a performance pattern in their many drills and maneuvers. These patterns are time-tested over months and years, and so new school children and recruits can be molded to the pattern quickly. The importance of performance pattern in the production of a play must be emphasized, because each play is new and different and not time-tested. Each day of rehearsal, each technical or dress rehearsal, and each tryout performance will see changes and refinements in the pattern until, in only a few days or possibly hours, the final pattern is set. The need for a good pattern is as important in the production of the play as in any other activity, but the limitation of time is more acute in the theater than in most other professions. Obviously any planning, any anticipation of production elements that facilitates the establishing of a good, strong performance pattern must be considered. These stage manager Clearing Houses are an excellent time to accomplish the groundwork for a good performance pattern.

The stage manager not only poses questions and finds answers; he must be attentive to those questions his assistants ask and, particularly, to answers or solutions they may propose. Many a fine technician has learned new methods by watching a duffer blunder through a problem to its solution. The assistants' questions also serve as a double-check to prevent overlooking the obvious.

b) Material Understudies. Many disasters or emergencies caused by breakage or mechanical failure can be avoided by having material or production understudies. Just as the actor has his understudy, the properties, lights, sound, etc. must have their understudies or alternates. Obviously a complete alternate production cannot be standing by, but any material thing, the loss or mechanical failure of which would upset the plot or smooth action of the play, must have an alternate. This is especially true of perishable, fragile, or intricate mechanical things. Such items as phone bells, cigarettes and matches, glassware, special spotlights, phonograph records, and flashlights are obvious examples. The most famous example is the cover gun held offstage, ready to fire in case the actor's gun misfires. These material understudies will be spotted when the stage managers are asking each other, "What do I do if ... ?" Arrangements should be made to have them prepared or manufactured by the appropriate production department.

FINAL DAILY CHECK LIST

1. Time and place of next rehearsal.
2. Time and place of appointments.
3. Status of actors on probation.
4. Changes of address.
5. Status of understudies.
6. Has Clearing House been held?
7. Is the prompt script up-to-date?
8. Diary.

REHEARSAL PROPERTIES

Only substitute rehearsal properties may be used during rehearsals, unless a property man has been hired. This is an IA (International Alliance of Theatrical Stage Employees and Motion Picture Operators of the United States and Canada—for obvious reasons called the IA or the Stage Hands Union) ruling and should not be violated.

A rehearsal prop is any simple makeshift that simulates the real prop but could not be construed to be the real prop. Paper cups are suitable rehearsal cocktail glasses; glassware of any sort might be construed to be the real thing and should not be used. A rolled newspaper is a suitable rehearsal substitute for a shiny, brass telescope; an old battered, black telescope is too close to the real thing—don't use it.

If a property man has been hired to handle a ground cloth for rehearsals, then he may be used for handling other properties, and all kinds of props, real or substitute, may be used.

In the event that an actor must read from a book or letter during the performance, the stage manager should receive instructions from the director as to whether or not the dialogue is to be inserted into the book so that the actor may actually read it. These props should be prepared by the stage managers to insure accuracy, and may be used at rehearsals.

READING REHEARSALS

In the foregoing portion on rehearsals it has been assumed that the director will want to start immediately with the actors "on their feet," with "walking rehearsals." However, many directors prefer to spend from one day to a week or more "reading the play." These readings are usually conducted by the director and are periods of intense concentration for discussion of characterizations, motivations and reading of lines. The stage manager will see that quiet is maintained and interruptions avoided.

Following the readings the actors will get on their feet, and rehearsals will proceed as described before. The actor will be advanced considerably in learning lines and characterization.

COLLATERAL REHEARSALS

When two or more rehearsals are in progress at the same time (as in a musical) the stage manager will spend most of his time with the "book" rehearsal. One assistant (usually the first assistant) will work with him in this rehearsal and be able to take over if the stage manager is called out of rehearsal. Another assistant will be present at the dance rehearsal and will make notes on new props, observe breaks, etc. The Information Exchange at the end of the day becomes especially important in these cases, as it is possible that none of the stage managers will have gotten the "complete picture" during the day.

One of the problems that will present itself in this situation is the use of actors who are required in both rehearsals at the same time. This can be forestalled by careful planning at the beginning of each day and by cooperation between the director and choreographer. The stage manager can help to secure this by presenting the conflict clearly. No one likes "surprises," but directors and choreographers will be able to plan their work around a performer if they know they have to.

The stage manager will have to plan special rehearsals, with the director's and/or choreographer's approval. As the choreographer and dance arranger complete their work, the orchestrator will be asked to come to rehearsal to see the dance in its more or less finished form. It is important that this be done as early as possible so that he may complete his orchestrations.

Other special rehearsals will include orchestra rehearsals with the company (orchestra readings will be dealt with by the music department), sound recordings and individual coaching, such as fencing lessons. They should be plotted carefully with the director and arrangements be made that other work may proceed, if they do not involve the entire company.

PART THREE

Rehearsals, Final Weeks

The final weeks of rehearsal see the fusion of the elements of production into a unified whole. These weeks constitute the stage manager's busiest and most creative of the production.

The following sections are broken down for purposes of study into roughly equal time periods. It must be borne in mind, however, that these time periods overlap and that the stage manager's chief function is to plan ahead.

THE RUN-THROUGH PERIOD

During the last stages of rehearsals, the director will have complete run-throughs of the play. The primary purposes of the run-through are to consolidate direction, establish tempo of the play as a whole, get a feeling of unity in the acting company and establish the playing time. If the early rehearsals have been held in a rehearsal hall, the director may wish the run-throughs to be held in a theatre. The general manager or company manager will arrange this, if he is able, and the stage manager will be responsible for transferring the rehearsal to the theatre. He must make arrangements for the stage to be marked and for rehearsal props to be transported to the theatre, and make sure that the company is aware of the new location and time of the call.

The run-through gives the stage manager and his assistants an opportunity to test and adjust the performance pattern they have planned and discussed during their Clearing Houses. It also offers them a chance to give the actors a preview of their cuing procedure.

The stage manager should try to approximate a performance atmosphere as completely as possible without scenery, costumes, lighting and properties. He will see that the actors receive proper warning calls, that all sound, light and other cues are given and that the effect is achieved or indicated; that an accurate record of the playing time is kept; and that a maximum number of rehearsal props are available and used. Although the director is occupied primarily with

67

acting during the run-through, it is desirable to incorporate into it as many of the special effects, costumes and properties as are legal and practicable. An actor should have as many opportunities to become familiar with these mechanics as is feasible.

An example of a "special" that may be incorporated into the run-through or earlier rehearsal is the use of pieces of cloth which actresses may pin to their street dresses to simulate trains. The costumer will furnish these trains, but the stage manager will take charge of them as he does substitute rehearsal properties.

The running time of each run-through and all technical and dress rehearsals should be entered in the diary. This information is useful for comparison purposes and is referred to frequently by all staff members.

I. Run-Throughs And The Staff. As soon as the director has determined when he will have run-throughs of the play, the stage manager should find out from him at which run-throughs the staff will be welcomed. These should be planned as far in advance as is practicable, as the staff can plan their time to be able to attend. It is the stage manager's job to make sure that the producer, the author, the designers and crew heads are told of the rehearsal. It should be emphasized that these are working sessions and that only essential personnel be allowed to attend.

The stage manager should also use his best efforts (tact is often the essence) to make sure that the staff not participate as an audience. Quite often the line that gets an enormous laugh in run-through lays an ostrich egg in performance.

For many of the staff this will be their first contact with the play other than as a manuscript. The stage managers must make themselves available to the designers and crew heads to answer questions and clarify business. If, for example, the property man sees an actor reading a tabloid-sized newspaper and he had counted on a full-sized newspaper, it is a small matter to adjust his property plot to clarify this. If, however, the designer and costume designer attest that such-and-such character cannot sit in a particular chair with the dress designed, the director should be consulted as to which of the three elements (chair, costume or staging) should be changed. Or, if the lighting designer sees dance movement that cannot possibly be lighted with the equipment he has planned, the choreographer should be apprised of this. If the choreographer is loathe to change his choreography and the lighting designer unwilling to spend more money for more equipment, the producer will have to arbitrate the matter.

If communication were perfect and time unlimited these questions would not arise. They are, however, inevitable. The stage manager, while ever avoiding "hubris," may permit himself and his staff a small self-congratulation if the surprises are at a minimum.

II. The Plots. The stage manager will continue to revise and elaborate the plots during this period. The Property Plot will be fairly near its final form. The Sound Plot will also be nearly frozen. It is at this point that the stage manager can number (or, rather, letter) the sound cues. Lettering (unless there are a very large number of sound cues) is preferable, as there will be no confusion with lighting cues, which will be numbered. The penciled notation of "Sound: Auto Horn" can be replaced with "Sound Cue D" (Auto Horn) in the prompt script. This is assuming that the sound tapes have been made and edited. The Electrics Plot will be sketchy and will contain only "demand cues." That is, cues which are indicated in the script or which have been requested by the director. They should not be numbered, but referred to by script page number. The prompt script should contain a notation of these cues in the margin with a brief description.

The Carpentry Plot will also be finalized during this time. It will contain the scenic elements used, scene by scene, and as much of the sequence of movement as is ascertainable at this time, and whatever is known about "blind changes," that is, scenic movements which will be made while a scene is playing in anticipation for a later change. It is valuable to indicate the time available for blind changes, plus any requirements that the change be held up while a quiet scene is playing on stage.

The designer will furnish the wardrobe mistress with a costume plot, but the stage manager should be prepared to supplement it if necessary. Understudies' costumes must be remembered.

III. Program Copy. The press agent is responsible for the composition of the program, but the aid of the stage manager is usually enlisted to check correctness of names of characters, names of actors, production credits and similar material.

IV. The Prompt Script. Mention was made previously that some time during rehearsals the stage manager stops "cleaning up" his prompt script. That time is now—when run-throughs start. By this time major dialogue or stage business changes have been made, and all future alterations should be small. If the stage manager has a "clean" script at the start of the run-throughs, there is a good chance that there will be no more than "word" changes until after the out-of-town opening.

This is not a hard and fast rule and there are exceptions, but the stage managers who follow this plan do so for the following reason. Within a few days after the run-throughs start, the stage manager will be away from rehearsals, concentrating on the setup. He will return to his prompt script only for technical and dress rehearsals. He will not have time to transfer his cues into a fresh manuscript or to familiarize himself with new pages sequences. When he returns to his prompt script, he will want it to fit like an old shoe. A new script could easily throw him out of the pattern he has been establishing. Obviously, if further major changes are made, a fresh typing of the section concerned may be necessary.

V. Understudy Progress. During all rehearsal periods the stage manager must not lose sight of the progress understudies are making. Check them constantly to see that they are keeping their dialogue and stage business up to date, that they are attending all rehearsals, that provisions have been made for their costuming, that they have learned their lines. Rehearse them when possible.

VI. Inspecting The Scenery. Some scenic studios have facilities for setting up the scenery in their shops, and they do so as a sort of preliminary setup and as a check against possible construction errors. Arrangements should be made for the actors to visit the studio and inspect the scenery while it is assembled, even though it may be unpainted. If possible this visit should be made before the run-throughs because added and concrete knowledge of the scenery will make the run-through considerably more real.

VII. Itinerary. A complete itinerary of the tryout tour should be made and a copy furnished to everyone in the production. This itinerary will include:

Dates of:

> Engagement, city, and theatre.
> Actors' trunk pick-up.
> Scenery pick-up.
> Plane or train departure and arrival time for crew.
> Plane or train departure and arrival time for cast.
> Rehearsal schedule, including type and kind.
> Performance dates and time, matinees and evenings.
> Photographing the production.

VIII. Hotel Reservations. At least two weeks before leaving New York for the out-of-town tryout the advance agent will furnish the stage manager with a list of hotels in the cities to be played. This list will include the names of hotels, types of accommodations, rates, and distance from the theatre. The stage manager will make these lists available to the actors and will press them to make reservations immediately, or at the latest, one week before leaving. Some actors prefer to make their own reservations. If not, it is the management's responsibility to make them for the actor. This is an Actors' Equity rule and was designed primarily to assist the touring actor when sudden shifts of schedule, or routing into crowded cities (and conventions seem to have a genius for happening in the city *your* show is playing in) are made by the management. If the actor relies on the management to get his hotel reservations, he must accept any reasonable accommodation offered, or pay for one night's lodging if he refuses the accommodation. It is understood that inability on the actor's part to get a reservation means that the actor cannot get *any* suitable accommodation, not that he cannot get the exact room, at the exact price, in the exact hotel he chooses. Thus it behooves the stage manager to keep after the actor and see that reservations are made early. Moreover, as trunks are carried in the scenery baggage cars, they will arrive at the tryout city one to several days before the actor, and the local transfer company must know where to deliver the trunks. Storage, at the actor's expense, is sometimes charged on undelivered trunks. Generally, managements are extremely co-operative in helping the actor get the hotel accommodation he desires. Nevertheless, making hotel reservations early is always good practice.

IX. Trunks. The management is required to transport actors' personal trunks from New York to the tryout cities and back. While wardrobe trunks are not in use as much as they once were, each member of the company should be asked if he plans to bring a trunk and the stage manager should prepare a list of trunks.

The stage manager will then furnish this list to the property man. The property man arranges with the transfer men to do the actual collecting of the trunks. The transfer companies generally limit their pickup area to central Manhattan and have specifications the actor must meet. The instruction given to the actor to have his trunk "ready and downstairs by nine o'clock" means just that. Transfer companies are not required to wait for last-minute packing, or to go above or below street level, to make a collection. Should the actor not meet the specifications for preparing his trunk for collection, and the trunk is left behind, it will be his responsibility to transport his trunk to the next city at his own expense.

If the actor lives outside the collection area, the management furnishes funds to enable the actor to have his trunk transported into the collection area; e.g., an actor living in Westchester may have his trunk checked into Grand Central Terminal at the management's expense (provided the cost is not more than six dollars), and then have the transfer people pick up the trunk from the Terminal. In this case the actor will turn over his claim check to the stage manager, who will attach it to the trunk pick-up list furnished the property man. It is advisable for the stage manager to keep a separate record of the claim check in case of loss.

All personnel in the production who use a trunk while touring receive the same consideration as the actor, and their names are included on all trunk lists.

Before the property man leaves for the next city, he should be furnished with a trunk delivery list, which he turns over to the transfer men at the next stand. This list has two parts—hotel trunks and theatre trunks. All hotel trunks are listed separately under actors' names, and the hotels to which they are to be delivered are indicated.

A new pickup list should be made by the stage manager for each city. This may be identical with the delivery list used on arrival, but often it is not. Actors have been known to shift hotels several times in the course of a week. The expense of shifting a trunk from hotel to hotel is borne by the actor. The management pays for *one* delivery and *one* pickup at each stand.

The management furnishes printeu hotel labels showing the name of the play and whether it is a hotel or theatre trunk. The actor should affix the proper one to his trunk. The press agent has these labels printed. He gives them to the stage manager, who distributes them to the actors and turns over the remaining supply to the property man.

X. Personnel Check-off List. The stage manager and his assistants should have a personnel check-off list. This list will include all personnel making the tryout tour and can be combined with the out-of-town address list. Such a list is useful for checking off the arrival of personnel at airports, meetings and rehearsals.

XI. Setup Schedule. The members of the staff will review that section of the production schedule having to do with the out-of-town setup. Refinements will be made, as by this time the crew will have been hired and their advice is invaluable. The stage manager will probably want to retype this part of the schedule (if substantial changes have been made) and distribute the revised setup schedule to all members of the production staff.

XII. Number of Stage Hands. The number of stage hands needed for the setup will be discussed by the staff members, and a call for them will be placed with the union local at the place of the setup. A discussion of the number of stage hands needed for dress rehearsals and performances will be found in Section Two of this part of the handbook.

73

XIII. O. P. (Opposite Prompt) Side. The prompt side of the stage will be determined by the permanent facilities of the theatre. Generally, the prompt side is the same side as the house switch board. It is usual to have the house switch board, the service feed (electrical service for the company boards), the house curtain control, and often, the pin rail on the same side. For obvious reasons of emergency cuing, the stage manager will place his prompt desk on the same side. He may have to change this procedure because of a lack of view of the stage, but in general this is a good plan. When developing his performance pattern and planning the assistants' duties during the performance, he will be thinking in terms of the New York theatre. If, however, the tryout theatres have facilities on the opposite side from the New York theatre, he must determine what problems arise from his being on a different side, solve them, and make sure that his assistants know about the problems and the solution. On most pre-Broadway tours this information will already be known to the stage manager. If it is not, a question to the production electrician will answer it for him.

XIV. Advice Sheet. An "advice sheet" will be delivered to the theatre manager of the out-of-town theatre. If an advance agent is employed (usually only on a long tour) he will deliver this in person. If not, the general manager, with the assistance of the company manager and press agent will make sure that it is in the hands of the theatre manager. Most of this information will consist of the press department's needs, program copy, marquee arrangements and publicity interviews. But it also contains technical information for the house crew of the theatre. Such things as spotted lines, traps to be cut in the stage floor, special electrics requirements, can be worked on days before the production arrives, thereby saving time on the setup.

It is often wise to have the production carpenter and/or the production electrician travel to the tryout town the week before the production moves in, to supervise this work. These arrangements will be made by the general manager, but the stage manager must keep himself informed.

XV. Technical Check List. Many days before leaving town the stage manager will begin making a list of technical questions which cannot be answered until the scenery is set up in the tryout theatre. Such things as sight line problems, physical limitations imposed by the theatre, and difficulties during scene shifts might comprise this list. When the director says, "We'll just have to wait until we get into the theatre to see how this works," the stage manager should make a note on his technical check list to check it out.

XVI. The Call. Several days before a company is to be transported to another city the company manager will post "the Call" or the call sheet. This is a standardized, printed form on which information is inserted pertaining to all personnel. This information includes:

Name of next stand (city).

Name of the theatre.

Number of matinee and evening performances to be played, their dates and times, and matinee days.

Time of train/plane departure and arrival and station for actors.

Time of train/plane departure and arrival and station for crew.

Date and time of hotel-trunk pickup.

Date, time, place baggage cars spotted at next stand.

Date, time of call at baggage cars for unloading.

Date, time of call at theatre to load in scenery.

Name and phone number of next stand's transfer company.

Time of orchestra rehearsal.

Hotel list for next stand. (Separate lists of hotels for several stands are usually furnished days or weeks in advance of posting the Call.)

Any special notes, such as time of call to interview extras.

Once posted on the call board, the Call may *not be removed by anyone* except the head production stage carpenter and/or the stage manager and company manager. The latter will remove it only to make changes. No one else, not even the producer, will remove the Call from the call board, even temporarily, for any reason.

After the final performance and after the production has been removed from the theatre, the head production carpenter is the last member of the company to leave the theatre. He is also the first to arrive at the new theatre, and so he will remove the Call and carry it with him for reference purposes. Sometimes, if the crew travels ahead of the acting company and the stage manager accompanies the crew, the carpenter will request that the stage manager carry the Call for safe-keeping. The stage manager will defer to the carpenter's wishes.

When leaving New York for its first tryout stand, the company will have been advised of the information on the Call days and weeks in advance of the actual posting of the Call. In this case its posting is something of an added formality. However, all future Calls at all future stands will be of vital interest to all personnel. The stage manager must see that inexperienced personnel familiarize themselves with it. It is the individual's responsibility thereafter to keep current with information pertinent to himself.

THE TRANSITION

The task of assembling the technical elements of the show now begins. The scenery will be loaded out of the scene shop, the electrics will be loaded out, the props, the trunks (including the wardrobe mistress' trunks or crates) the costumes, and if the show has an orchestra, heavy musical instruments and the boxes or crates containing the scores. (The stage manager can serve as liaison between the property man, who will be responsible for transporting the music department's equipment, and the contractor, who will be responsible for it at each end of the trip.)

The stage manager will turn over the running of the cast rehearsals to his assistants and will spend most of his time in the theatre where the setup is being made. In the case of an out-of-town tryout tour, the original setup is usually made in the theatre of the first stand. The stage manager will travel with the technical staff, preceding the acting company by one or several days. In this handbook it is presumed that a tryout tour is being made.

I. Work Schedule. Plan a work schedule with the production crew heads and the company manager and keep a time sheet of the crew's working hours. Insist on proper rest periods and meal hours.

II. House Physician. Determine how to locate and obtain the services of the house physician quickly.

76

III. Additional Rehearsal Space. If the first tryout stand is relatively close to New York City, the acting company will remain in New York while the setup is being made and will time its arrival at the tryout stand to coincide with the completion of the setup. Then technical and dress rehearsals will start immediately. However, at future stands, or if the acting company accompanies the scenery and technical staff, rehearsal space other than the stage of the theatre must be provided, because the stage will be utilized for setup purposes. Theatre lobbies and smoking rooms are used if available and large enough. Ballrooms and dining rooms in near-by hotels are alternate choices, as are empty theatres, if the tryout city should have them. Fraternal organizations have meeting halls they sometimes rent for such purposes. The local theatre manager will have suggestions. As these extra rehearsal spaces are often rented, the problem should be discussed with the company manager before the stage manager leaves New York, since the company manager will pay the bill.

IV. Assigning Dressing Rooms. It should be remembered that dressing rooms are assigned with the best interests of the production in mind. Prestige, prejudice and whim are secondary. If there are contractual agreements between the actor and management concerning dressing rooms, the general manager will advise the stage manager of such agreements. Normally the assignment of dressing rooms solves itself easily.

Keeping in mind the following factors for each actor, the stage manager should have no difficulty: the proximity of the dressing room to the stage, or the side of the stage on which it is located, is important to actors with many costume changes, or with a quick change not made on stage. Age and sex of the actor; location of toilets, showers, and washrooms; size, ventilation and anterooms; and condition of the dressing room itself are all factors to be considered. Generally speaking, if there are two actors of equal importance to the production, and one is a woman, she will have the better dressing room.

If there is no wardrobe room, a dressing room should be assigned the wardrobe mistress as a workroom.

A list of dressing room assignments should be posted on the call board. Copies should be given to the wardrobe mistress to expedite distribution of costumes and to the production property man for a guide in distributing the actors' theatre trunks.

The dressing rooms should be checked for cleanliness, lights, mirrors, chairs, hangers, toilet facilities and keys to lock doors. Changes needed in chairs and carpets should be reported to the house property man, lighting changes to the house electrician and faulty locks to the house carpenter.

V. Prompt Desk. Place the prompt desk, allowing sufficient room for prompting and cuing. Locate and test all cuing devices.

VI. Supervision of Departments. The stage manager must be available at all times during the setup. In general he works through his production chiefs when giving suggestions or corrections to individual stage hands. This is common sense delegation of authority and responsibility, but in the heat of activity it may be neglected. It should not be. Much of the stage manager's time will be spent answering questions from members of the different departments. Some typical problems the stage manager may face, and a list of personnel involved, follow:

1. CARPENTRY DEPARTMENT. Placing portable dressing rooms, practicality of scenery, sight lines, masking, cross-overs, safety.

   The production carpenter is known as "the carpenter," and his assistant is often the flyman. Members of the carpentry department are under the house carpenter and are called "grips."

2. PROPERTY DEPARTMENT. Arrangement of props onstage, placement of small props, preparation of edibles, identification of props.

   Production property man is "the property man." House property man has charge of the "clearers" or "handlers."

3. ELECTRICAL DEPARTMENT. Positions of onstage fixtures and switches. Location of special spots. Number and position of work lights.

   Production electrician is "the electrician." The house electrician has charge of the "operators."

4. WARDROBE DEPARTMENT. Identification of costumes and accessories.

Sometimes the wardrobe mistress needs assistance in preparing costumes and hires members of the local union. They are often called "wardrobe women" (or men), and, if they assist actors to change their costumes, they are called "dressers." These are separate from the actors' personal servants, who are usually known as "maids" or "valets."

Make arrangements to protect the actors' costumes from damage or dirt backstage. The backstage area is often dirty, especially during technical and dress rehearsals. The best solution is to get the area cleaned, but the pressure of time may not allow this. Also floors, narrow passageways and cross-overs can never be made spotless. The use of cloths on the floor and on walls and particularly around stage machinery will help protect costumes. Duplicate sets of cloths should be available, so that replacements are on hand when one set is being laundered.

5. SOUND DEPARTMENT. Locate equipment, test effects, get volumes and establish cuing procedure.

6. GENERAL. Try to get the answers for technical check list prepared during run-throughs.

VII. Lighting. The lighting designer's work will cover three broad areas:

a. The placement of each instrument and the switches used to control each instrument. He will have made these decisions long before the show is loaded out of New York and his work will be recorded on two documents, the "hanging plot" and the "board hook-up chart." If the designer employs an assistant, the assistant will be in charge of these documents and will keep them up to date. (Changes are inevitable.) If the designer does not employ an assistant, this work will probably devolve upon the stage manager. In any event the stage manager should familiarize himself with the hanging and switch set-up of the show..

b. The focusing and framing of each instrument. Usually the designer has made some notes on where each lamp is to "play," but his information is not formalized. The assistant will keep a "focus chart"

NO.	CIRC.	COLOR	TYPE-WATT	AREA	#1 PIPE	
					FOCUS	FRAMING
1	7	517	L 500	6	8'L. of #2 PORTAL	OPEN R./OFF STAIRS/OFF CYC/OPEN D.S.
2	8	82	L 500	5	2'L. of C.-EVEN W/#2 PORT.	EDGE OF STAIRS/OFF CYC/OPEN D.S.
3	21	219	F 500	4	3'R. of #2 L. PORT.	HARD FOCUS
4	7	517	L 500	6	6'L. of #2 PORTAL	OPEN R./ OFF STAIRS / OFF CYC./ OPEN D.S.
5	8	82	L 500	5	C.-EVEN of #2 PORT.	EDGE OF STAIRS R&L./ OFF CYC./ OPEN D.S.
6	21	219	F 500	4	5'R. of #2L. PORT.	HARD FOCUS
7	7	517	L 500	6	4'L. of #2R. PORT.	OFF PORT./OPEN L./OFF CYC./ OPEN D.S.
8	8	82	L 500	5	2'R. of C.-EVEN of #2PORT.	EDGE OF STAIRS R&L./OFF CYC./ OPEN D.S.
9	21	219	F 500	4	7'R. of #2L. PORT.	HARD FOCUS
10	7	517	L 500	6	2'L. of #2R. PORT.	OFF PORT./OPEN L. /OFF CYC./ OPEN D.S.
ETC.						
ETC.						
ETC.						

and, again, if no assistant is employed, the stage manager will assume that function. On page 80 is a suggestion as to the kind of chart to be used to record the focusing and framing. The stage manager will also be on hand to advise the lighting designer of staging requirements that must be met and to answer questions concerning the staging of the play in general. It should be noted here that most IATSE locals require that the entire take-in crew be kept on until the focusing is completed. Since most of the other departments will have completed their work, it is obvious that the focusing must be done with as little delay as possible.

c. The lighting of the show. That is, the determination by the designer of which instruments are in use at any particular time. Each time different instruments come into play it is a new cue, and should be written in the prompt script. The stage manager will have provided the designer with the lighting plot containing the "demand cues" and he will assist in questions of staging, etc. Again, if an assistant is not present, it may be up to the stage manager to keep a record of these cues. The "master cue sheet" on page 82 can be useful.

VII. Scenery. After the production carpenter has hung the show, he will become interested in the sequence of scenic moves. The stage manager should provide him with the most up-to-date Scenery Plot and provide him with enough copies for his assistants. He will get a chance to understand the scenery movement during the lighting session, as he will probably be required to provide each set in sequence as it is lit. The designer or his assistant will, of course, be present to check that the scenery is positioned correctly. Likewise, the property man will be required to position the major "set" props. This is an ideal time for marking the positions of the props.

VIII. Orchestras. If an orchestra is to be used in the pit or backstage, arrange for its accommodation.

The management may not plan to use a pit orchestra in New York and may not wish one on the road, but very often theatres in tryout cities have contracts with the local musicians, who will play willy-nilly! Sometimes the management will welcome a pit orchestra. In any event the music to be played should be decided. This sometimes falls to the stage manager. He should arrange a meeting with the orchestra leader,

81

CUE# →	PRE-SET	③ 1	⑥ 2	⑧ 3	③ 4	⑧ 5	⑫ 6	⑧ 7
SWITCH# ↓								
1		F					↓5	
2		F					↓5	
3				↑3				↓0
4							↑3	
5		F	↓7		↑F			
6		F	↓7		↓0			
7	F		↓0					
8	F		↓0					
9		F						
10			↑3					
11	F							
12						↑F		
13	3							
14								
15								
16								
ETC. ↓								

The numbers in circles indicate the number of counts (seconds) in which the cue is executed.

82

at which time the music to be used, the length of the overture and intermission music, and methods of cuing can be decided.

IX. Stage Crew Run-Through. Before the full technical or dress rehearsals which include actors, a run-through for the stage crews should be held. The complexity of the production will decide whether or not this should be done by all crews simultaneously or by each department singly. During this run-through, all shifts of scenery, sound cues, lighting changes and cues, placement and disposal of properties, and curtain cues must be accomplished. All mechanical adjustments may be made without the distraction that a company of actors brings. It should be remembered that the stage crew must adjust itself in a very few days to a new play that the playwright, producer, director, designers and actors have taken months to devise. The stage manager must help make this adjustment painless.

The stage manager will be most helpful to the production stage crew if he acts as a general overseer rather than concentrates on one particular department. He can assign his assistants as overseers of individual parts of the scene change. During scene shifts his traditional observation post is Downstage Center, facing Upstage with his back against the house curtain. In this position he is out of the way and can observe all departments simultaneously and can gather material to help coordinate the change.

The stage manager must plan where the actor is to wait during the changes, where to go after an exit and where to wait for entrance cues. If he is alert to the idiosyncracies of the technical end of the production, he is better equipped to watch over the welfare and safety of all backstage personnel.

X. Performance Check List. The stage manager does not have time to check every item involved in a quick change of scenery. He makes a special "performance check list" for use during the performance, especially just before ringing up the curtain on a scene. This list is small and includes just those items that vitally concern the plot or business during the ensuing scene. These things are most often properties, but will include lighting equipment, costumes, and the scenery. If these items are prepared and in place, the performance may proceed; without

83

them there is no performance; e.g., the revolver in the desk drawer, with which the hero shoots the villain, *must be in place and prepared* or the show goes out the window; the antimacassar on the chair is decorative and indicative of character, but its absence in no way interrupts the plot or action. The revolver is on the list, the antimaccassar is not. Again, the door D.R. *must be open* so that the hero can see the villain's approach; the door U.L. to a closet may be open or shut, and it will not concern the play vitally. The door D.R. is on the list, the door U.L. is not. This list should be kept as small as possible. Its contents are much the same as the "material understudies" mentioned previously but are not necessarily identical.

XI. Personnel Watching Setup. Actors and other production members should not be discouraged from watching the setup. The desire to watch the progress of "their" production is a healthy sign and should be encouraged. However, make sure that all watchers keep out from under foot and do their watching from a safe place. The stage manager is responsible for the safety of all persons backstage. Accidents are rare, and the producer carries insurance to protect personnel *who have a legitimate reason* for being backstage. This does not include wives, sweethearts or the doorman's great-aunt Sue. Should an unauthorized person be involved in an accident, the stage manager is in an awkward situation.

XII. Fireproofing. Scenery, draperies, and other properties obtained through reputable theatrical supply houses are automatically fireproofed (more properly, the term is flameproofed). This is in the business manager's province, but is on the stage manager's list of Things Not To Be Forgotten.

During the setup in each city played, an inspector from the local fire department may examine all inflammable articles and test them with an open flame, often a lighted match but sometimes a red-hot blowtorch. An article that does not pass inspection must be flameproofed before a performance may be given. While on tour, the stage manager will see that the firm or individual doing the flameproofing furnishes a dated and signed certificate or affidavit describing the articles treated and affirming that the treatment has been accomplished.

Open flames on the stage must be circumvented by some means. The fire departments in many cities will not permit them. Electric substitutes for candles, oil lamps and fires in fireplaces have been in use for so long that audiences accept them as conventional stage effects.

In some cities open flames are permitted, but only with a permit of the local fire department. The house property man in the theatre played will usually know the fire regulations and will know whom to get in touch with to obtain a permit.

Onstage ashtrays should contain a film of water so that lighted cigarettes will not smolder. Exits should be equipped with water or sand buckets in which lighted cigarettes may be doused when carried offstage by actors.

Fire inspectors are serious-minded, responsible individuals. Evidence of fire-prevention equipment and precautions will gain the inspector's respect and cooperation. Carelessness or disregard of precautions may lead to severe penalties.

XIII. Children And Animals. The use of children or animals in a production must be approved by local city departments and societies. Arrangements for approval are made by the general manager in New York City and by the advance agent on the road; but this, too, is one of the things the stage manager must have on his list of Things Not To Be Forgotten. In general, the various Gerry societies that handle this matter are very cooperative, but arrangements take time. The child's background, home life, health, family finances and schooling must be investigated; the animal's health, transportation, quartering and feeding must be approved. Any last-minute attempt to rush through a permit will be looked upon with suspicion by the authorities.

ASSEMBLING ALL ELEMENTS

At this point all the technical elements and all the acting elements are brought together. Whether this meeting of the elements results in a loud collision or a quiet fusing depends in large measure on how well the stage manager has done his planning.

Technical rehearsals differ from the stagecrew run-through in that they include actors. The technical rehearsal aims to coordinate the technical and acting departments of the production, and time is taken to correct errors. Sometimes whole scenes are repeated. Dress rehearsals, on the other hand, are really performances, and an attempt is made to progress through the play without stopping, even though the production may falter badly at times.

Technical rehearsals normally include all elements of the production, but emphasis is on mechanics rather than acting. The stage manager will try to run both technical and dress rehearsals as nearly like performances as possible. As managing the performance is taken up in detail in Part Four, only added suggestions for technicals rehearsals are made here.

I. Schedule. Plan a schedule and stick to it.

II. Taking Charge. The stage manager is now in charge, and he must assume full control. To be in charge and remain in charge, the stage manager must not be distracted from his post at the prompt desk.

It seems inevitable that at the exact moment the stage manager is forced to abandon his prompt script some actor needs a prompt. This is not necessarily Fate playing a cruel trick. The break in routine, or performance pattern, that has distracted the stage manager may be the same thing that has upset the actor. The stage manager must learn to override these distractions and keep his primary focus onstage.

The greatest distraction, dividing his attention to answer questions, can be reduced if backstage personnel are trained to address their questions to the assistant. The importance of well-trained, well-briefed assistants looms larger!

III. Irregularities. Advise the actors of all technical idiosyncracies and unforeseen production elements discovered during the setup.

IV. Maintaining Quiet. Personnel will be tired, nerves will be raw, tempers short.

V. Making Corrections. Work as quickly as possible, but take time to correct and adjust. Don't be stampeded! A mistake must be understood to be corrected. When a difficult cue or scene change is approaching, it is advisable to stop the rehearsal, explain the problem to crew and actors, explain the solution to the problem, and then proceed to attempt the solution after everyone understands his part. The stage manager, of course, has analyzed these problems from the day he first read the manuscript, has investigated them during the setup, and will be prepared with the solution. These interruptions to correct or avoid errors will save confusion and time, and possibly accidents. Remember, the shin you avoid cracking may be your own!

VI. Performance Pattern. Try to consolidate and set performance pattern during these rehearsals. Repetition forms habits; be sure these performance habits are good ones.

The performance pattern for the stage managers will have been fully prepared if the stage manager has been conscientious in his training program. Now he can use his time and energy to adjust and refine the pattern.

VII. Cutting Dialogue. At technical rehearsals, if the production is complicated by many scenes, costumes and cues, try to have the director agree to cutting out all unnecessary dialogue. By doing so, the stage manager can jump from cue to cue, using only enough dialogue to lead into the cue or time the change. Be sure not to short-change anyone, though. If dialogue is out before off-stage costume changes and prop sets, are completed, there will be no saving of time. If dialogue is cut judiciously, a great deal of time and energy can be saved. Usually directors are agreeable to this method of conducting technical rehearsals, since the constant interruptions for adjustments militate against smooth acting performances.

VIII. Many managements provide the stage manager with formal printed forms for reporting the data about the show. Whether they do or not, the thoughtful stage manager will make this information available to the management. On page 88 is a suggested form to report this information.

Another type of timing which should be kept is the time necessary to accomplish scene changes. This information can be kept in the stage manager's prompt script. The time consumed for scene changes during technical rehearsals will not necessarily remain unchanged. As the crew gets more practice with the changes the time in which they are made will be cut down.

_____ COMPANY

STAGE MANAGER

STAGE MANAGER'S DAILY REPORT

Eve

197 _____ Mat. Perf. No. _____

Running Time:	Technical Notes:
I	
II	
III	
Total Running Time:	
Total Elapsed Time:	
Late:	Absent:
Replacements/Understudies:	Notices: Given/Received:
Accident/Injuries:	Rehearsal/WorkSchedule:
Performance Notes:	

_____

Stage Manager

Referred to earlier was the rule of thumb that a page of dialogue runs on an average of one minute. But this is only a rule of thumb. During dress rehearsals the stage manager should begin marking times in his book. If the show is timed with a stop watch (a wise procedure) it is a small matter to glance at the elapsed time on the watch and mark it opposite a line of dialogue—preferably at the beginning and ending of a scene. This has two functions. First, the stage manager can tell if a scene begins to slow down later in the run. (This should not be the only yardstick used in judging the quality of the performance, needless to say!) Second, it may be possible that the director, playwright or producer might want to see only a specific scene. The stage manager, by a glance at his book, will be able to discover the scene begins, say, thirty-three minutes after the curtain goes up.

IX. Curtain Calls. Rehearse all curtain calls. The director will establish these. Sometimes removing backings and rearranging furniture speeds up the calls. The stage manager will co-ordinate this. Curtain calls are part of the performance pattern and should be established as such.

X. Orchestras. Ordinarily pit orchestras are not used at technical rehearsals. Musical productions usually have the conductor and a pianist in the pit for technical rehearsals, very often a special technical rehearsal with the full orchestra, and the full orchestra at dress rehearsals. The cuing procedures among the stage managers will have been worked out and tried during the technical rehearsals. The conductor will have rehearsed the orchestra separately. Any cuing problems among stage manager, conductor and performers will have been solved by dress rehearsal. The primary thing to remember is that technical or dress rehearsals with full crew and orchestra are incredibly expensive. It is irritating and wasteful to spend an inordinate amount of time on a problem which could have been solved beforehand.

An onstage orchestra is a production element and is included in all technical and dress rehearsals.

XI. Rest Periods. If the rehearsals are at night and will be long, plan a rest period and have refreshments brought in for everyone. (Don't neglect stage hands and others.) A half-hour spent this way will save hours lost through fatigue.

XII. Determining Number of Stage Hands. The number of stage hands to be used in performance and for the touring setups, performances, and taking down is determined during the initial setup and during technical and dress rehearsals. The stage manager with his on-the-scene advantage will be expected to have concrete ideas on this matter. The actual number of hands used will be decided by the company manager and the business agent of the Stage Hands Union Local at the place of the first setup and performances. Others consulted will be the house crew heads, the production crew heads and the stage manager.

Understaffing, presuming the local business agent is asleep (which he is not!), is poor economy. Inefficient backstage conditions result in poor morale, which, in turn, is reflected in poor performance. Also, the chance of accident is increased. Overstaffing is as senseless in the theatre as in any business and results in a shortened life for the production. A well-balanced, efficient crew should be the goal. This should be remembered: the Stage Hands Union will not object to additions to the stage crew, but it will object strenuously to attempts to reduce the crew after the minimum number has been determined. In fact, reduction of the minimum crew is never permitted unless concrete evidence of elimination or simplification of some physical elements of the production is submitted. During the technical and dress rehearsals, the stage manager, in conjunction with the production crew heads, submits to the producer, director, and designer a maximum number of suggestions for eliminations or simplifications of elements of physical production.

Once determined, the minimum crew call is sent to the Stage Hands Union Local in each city to be played by means of the "yellow card." The yellow card, so named because of its color, is a card of three sections furnished by the local secretary of the Stage Hands Union to the production's head carpenter. One section is filled out and sent to the local secretary at the next stand; another section is mailed to the general business office of the IA; the third section is retained by the production carpenter and is delivered by him to a representative of the union at the next stand. The card conveys the following information: the names of the production crew heads and the number of production hands in each department; the number of local stage hands needed in each department to take in the production, run the performance, put out the production, and to load and unload the baggage cars. The stage manager will not handle the stage hands' yellow card, but he must know the information it contains.

PHOTOGRAPHING THE PRODUCTION

A preliminary meeting of photographer, press agent, director, designers, company manager and stage manager should be held to plan:
1. The time and place to take the pictures.
2. The number, type, and subject of the pictures to be taken.

Using the information obtained at the above meeting, a shooting schedule should be composed which will take into consideration the following:
1. Eliminate unnecessary moving of camera (long and short shots).
2. Eliminate unnecessary changing of scenery.
3. Eliminate unnecessary changing of costumes.
4. Make quick use of and dismiss seldom used or not used actors and other personnel.

The schedule itself is a list of the pictures in shooting sequence and includes:
1. Name of the picture (indicative dialogue or business).
2. Type of shot (long, medium, or close-up).
3. Actors required for each picture.
4. A reminder after each picture of actors free to make costume change, or no longer needed and ready for dismissal.

A copy of the schedule is provided for the director, the photographer, the press agent, and the stage manager.

Company picture calls made during the rehearsal period are a part of the rehearsal hours. If calls are made after an out-of-town or New York opening, and are held after a performance, they must not exceed three hours from the time of the final curtain.

91

Having opened out-of-town, the production now goes into its final testing period. (We will assume, for discussion, that a pre-Broadway tour is scheduled. Many shows have opened recently in New York after previews there. The problems are generally the same; however, certain union rules are different. A digest of these rules will be found in the appendix.) The pre-Broadway tryout will give the producer, director, playwright, composer and choreographer a chance to view their work and make whatever changes they deem necessary. Very often these changes are extensive. The stage manager must make sure that the changes are smoothly assimilated into the production.

I. Rehearsal Space. During the transition period the stage manager will have lined up possible rehearsal space. He will also, with the help of the company manager, make sure that pianos, if they are needed, will be rented and moved to the space he has obtained. The space needs will, of course, vary depending upon the size of the production and the facilities of the theatre. The stage manager will have to anticipate the needs and act accordingly.

II. Rehearsal Time. Actors' Equity rules provide for a seven-day week and a "ten out of twelve hour" rehearsal period daily while on a pre-Broadway tour. Allowing for a 3½-hour performance, this leaves 6½-hours of rehearsal time each day. (Matinee days, 3 hours.) The five hour maximum span obtains as does the 1½-hour meal break. An out-of-town rehearsal schedule might read:

12 Noon until 5 pm -- Rehearsal
5 pm until 6:30 pm -- Meal Break
6:30 pm until 8 pm -- Rehearsal
8 pm until 8:30 pm -- Half-hour
8:30 pm until 11:30 pm -- Performance

In the above example, however, it might be unwise to attempt to rehearse between 7:30 pm and 8:00 pm, as the stage crew will use this time to check out the lights, scenery and props on the stage and the property department will have the stage mopped during this time (a necessity to protect costumes). If new material is to go into the show, this may be the only time during the day when the stage manager can outline the changes to the production staff. The house manager of the theatre will also want to use this time to make sure that the theatre staff is ready to open the house (usually at 8 pm). On top of that many actors, particularly those with difficult make-up problems, wish to use this time to prepare for the performance. Most experienced directors realize these problems and rarely attempt to rehearse within an hour of the half-hour call.

Another factor which the stage manager must take into consideration is whether the house crew is needed during rehearsal. Union rules vary from city to city. If, in the above schedule, the house crew must be present if the company rehearses on stage, the hours between Noon and 1 pm may be penalty hours and exorbitantly expensive for rehearsal.

The stage manager must familiarize himself with the rehearsal conditions and be ready to assist the director in determining the rehearsal calls.

III. New Material. During the out-of-town tryout new material will be constantly added to the show. The cardinal rule for all additions to or deletions from the show is that they be approved by the director. The stage manager will often be besieged by everyone from the producer's wife to the stage doorman to change the performance in one way or another. He must turn a polite, but deaf ear to these suggestions and refer the person with the suggestion to the director. He may, if asked, make his own suggestions, but only to the director! He should discourage "Monday morning quarterbacking" among the staff.

Once new material has been approved, the stage manager operates precisely as he did when he originally "broke down" the script. Since he is familiar with the rest of the show, he can break down the new material by means of a check list:

1. Contradictions: Does the new scene conflict with any factual information in the rest of the play? Is Character A required to be ninety years old in the new scene when he is seventeen in the rest of the play? These problems should be brought to the attention of the director, who will solve them with the playwright.

2. Actors: Are there additional characters in the new scene? Who is to play them?

3. Costumes: Are new or additional costumes required? Who is to build them? When will they be delivered? Has the costume designer been apprised of the change? Have the actors sufficient time for costume changes?

4. Scenery: Is new scenery required? When will it be delivered? If existing scenery is to be used, will the new scene affect scenery changes? Are there "impossible" scenery changes required? (If there are "impossible" changes involved, the stage manager should, of course, report it to the director. He will be wise, however, if he consults with the master carpenter first and tries to come up with an acceptable alternative for the director's consideration.)

5. Props: Are additional props required? Is the designer and/or property man aware of the exact requirements? When will the new props be ready?

6. Lighting: Is new lighting required? Is the lighting designer or his assistant aware of exactly what is needed? (If the lighting designer is unavailable, the stage manager may make minor adjustments in the lighting. These will be understood to be temporary and the stage manager should keep notes on what was changed to give to the lighting designer when he again appears. The stage manager should never attempt major changes and never, never refocus the instruments.)

7. Music: If music is added to the show, when will the orchestrations be ready? Is the copyist standing by? When will the orchestra rehearse the new music? These problems will be solved by the music department, but they must be coordinated with the stage manager.

IV. Running Order. In multi-scene shows a running order should be made up and printed on large (36" by 24") cards and posted on each side of the backstage area where they can be referred to by all backstage personnel. As thus:

ACT I

Sc. 1 – WILLIE'S LIVING ROOM

Sc. 2 — 72ND STREET
Sc. 3 — MUSEUM
Sc. 4 — RESTAURANT
Sc. 5 — 72ND STREET
Sc. 6 — "HIP HIP HOORAY" NUMBER
Sc. 7 — DOCTOR'S OFFICE

If the running order is changed, new cards should be made up and posted in place of the old ones. A change of running order will raise many of the same questions for the stage manager that new material will, particularly with respect to the scenery changes, lights, props, and costume changes.

On a day that new material goes into the show, or the running order is changed, the stage manager should apprise the technical departments as early in the day as possible so that they may begin whatever adjustments are necessary. If the changes are major, the technical departments may need several days to prepare for them. The stage manager will set a time to meet with the crew heads and their assistants to go over the routine of the evening's performance. The stage manager will probably detail one of his assistants to meet with the property man and another to meet with the wardrobe mistress, while he deals with the carpenter and the master electrician. Many productions employ a follow spot man (or men) with whom communication is difficult or impossible during the performance. They must be apprised of changes also. Since the master electrician will probably have a great deal of work to do changing cue sequences, the stage manager should deal with the follow spot man directly. Very often the exact nature of the changes is not set until the end of the rehearsal day. The stage manager has, then, from that time until curtain up to incorporate the changes into the evening's performance. It can easily be seen why the stage manager's pre-Broadway diet is heavy with take-out sandwiches and "cardboard" coffee. Seemingly minor changes can affect every member of the backstage staff. The director who insists on changes within an hour of curtain time is driving his stage manager into early retirement.

After half-hour the cast should review with the stage manager the changes in the performance. The stage manager may do this review one of several ways. If the changes affect only a few actors, he may review them in the actors' dressing rooms. If they affect most of the cast, he may utilize the dressing room speaker system, or (better) gather the company on stage before "places" is called and review the changes then. At these times it is important that he appear calm and in control. If the stage manager sounds rattled or disorganized, the company will catch his nervousness (the most contagious disease in the theatre) and will give a rattled performance.

If practical, it is customary to review with the star alone in his dressing room. This will permit the star to use the time when the stage manager is reviewing with the company to concentrate on the performance at hand without the strain of last minute instructions "from the bench."

It is possible that the conductor will have to use part of the time with the cast to review musical changes. The stage manager should have gotten any problems sorted out with the conductor before this time.

Again, it is highly important that material deleted from the script be saved. Audiences in New Haven, Boston, Philadelphia and Toronto have seen thousands of scenes which appeared in shows for only one or two performances before they were replaced by the original scene.

PART FOUR

Managing The Performance

BEFORE THE OPENING CURTAIN

1. The acting company should be called to the theatre in the afternoon or early evening for a rehearsal when it is known that an understudy will appear in a major role. An understudy appearing in a small role need not require the company to rehearse with. His appearance will probably affect only one or two characters in the play and if rehearsal is required, it can be done at half-hour.

2. All stage managers should be in the theatre before the half-hour call, under any circumstances.

3. Before the house curtain has been lowered and the auditorium opened to the audience, have:

    a. the front lights been checked?

    b. all sound effects been tested?

4. The Half-hour Call

    a. Are all actors and understudies in the theatre? If not, start locating them immediately. Here is an instance for which an up-to-date address list is necessary.

    There are many ways of making the half-hour and other calls and checking the actors. In some productions a check-in list is posted on the call board, and the actor is expected to register his arrival. Some theatres have elaborate signal systems to each dressing room. Most managers prefer to have the call made by an assistant, who personally checks the presence of each actor. Just as Mechanical cuing systems are subject to failure, mechanical calling systems have their drawbacks, too. The personal method of making calls assures the stage manager that the actor is in the theatre, because the assistant *sees* him; assures him that the actor knows that the call has been made, because a manager has *personally told him.*

    b. If any actor is missing, advise the understudy and wardrobe mistress immediately.

    c. See that all visitors leave the backstage area at this time.

Sometimes there are visitors backstage who are there for legitimate reasons. An artist, sketching the backstage elements of the production while it is in progress, is an example. Be sure that all actors understand why this visitor is there. A stranger in the wings has the same effect on an actor as someone peering over his shoulder while he is writing a personal letter.

    d. After checking in, no actor should leave the backstage area without permission from the stage manager.

    e. Check the setting of the first scene. Check to see that all doors, windows, drapes, etc., function properly. Check all properties for the first scene and, as far as possible, all props that can be present for ensuing scenes.

    f. Give notes on the performance, based on either the stage manager's or the director's previous viewing of the show. Many directors watch the show regularly and sometimes use the stage manager to transmit their corrections to the cast. If notes from either source are elaborate or complicated, the stage manager will call the actors involved to the theatre early to rehearse the scene. It should be remembered, however, that the time between seven-thirty and eight is a busy one on stage, what with the electrician checking the front circuits and the property man mopping the stage. The crew should be warned if a rehearsal is planned, so that they may work around it.

5. The Fifteen-Minute Call

    a. If an actor is still missing and unaccounted for, make definite arrangements for the understudy to go on. Be sure all actors are alerted to the situation.

Advise the company and house managers, and arrange that an announcement to the audience be made at the proper time. Actors' Equity requires that the announcement be made in the following manner:

A posted announcement (on a card at least eight by ten inches) at the entrance of the theatre within sight of anyone entering where the ticket taker stands. The name of

98

the role and the name of the actor must be in letters at least one-inch high. Very often the press department can be induced to secure a display sign which reads:

At This Performance
The Role of

Will Be Played By

The blanks are slots which receive strips of cardboard on which are printed the name of the character and the name of the actor. In a long-running show the stage manager will have strips on which are printed the name of each understudy and each character.

The above described posted announcements *must* be done.

Equity also requires one of two following:

1. An Announcement (usually made by the stage manager) from the stage just before the rise of the curtain or the start of the overture. This announcement is usually made on the speaker system with a microphone at the stage manager's desk.

Or,

2. Printed slips inserted into the program. It is the stage manager's responsibility to turn these slips over to the house manager for his staff to insert them in each program.

It is a wise stage manager who checks that they are inserted.

Be sure to inform the crew that an understudy will appear. The crew can be very helpful to the understudy during shifts, with the arrangements of props, etc.

b. Receive information concerning exact time to start the performance. Heavy rainstorms and other elements delay the arrival of audiences, and it is usually advisable to postpone starting beyond the scheduled time.

c. Begin composing the riot act to be read to the actor. who has been thoughtless enough to miss the half-hour call and the

99

fifteen-minute call and not called in to the theatre to report that he is either on his way or ill. It is unforgivable for an actor to regard his profession so lightly that he thinks it makes no difference to the show whether he is present or not.

6. The Five-Minute Call
   a. All necessary stage hands, particularly the house electrician and the curtain man, should be in the theatre.
   b. Check Carpenter, Props, and Electrics. Are all departments ready to go?
   c. If an understudy is to appear, check the wardrobe department. Has the understudy been provided with all necessary costumes or substitutes? If a different costume is to appear in the show, have the other actors seen it? Often the appearance of a new costume will destroy actors' concentration. Make sure there are no surprises.
   d. Ring the lobby signal (act-warning bell).
   e. Receive permission from the company manager to start. (Usually necessary only when the curtain has been delayed.)
   f. Check with conductor. Is the orchestra ready to start? (The conductor usually uses the time between the fifteen-minute call and the five-minute call to give notes to the musicians and solve orchestral problems.)
   g. Final check, using performance check list.
7. "Places" Call

It is customary to check with the production's star before calling, "Places, please." It is easy to postpone the opening curtain at this point. Any delay or stalling after "Places" has been called will be difficult and aggravating.

"Places, please" means that everyone involved in the production should assume his usual post to begin the show. It is a courtesy, however, to make a separate call for the orchestra to enter the pit. Then, another call for the conductor to enter.

At the proper time, start the performance. The opening sequence will vary according to the type of show and the cues the stage manager is obliged to give. The following is a model only, and illustrates one possible opening sequence:

a. House To Half (To house electrician)

The house electrician responds, "House at half," when he has accomplished the cue. This may be a cue (pre-arranged with the conductor) to start the overture.

b. Preset (To production electrician)

This should be asked for in sufficient time before the completion of the overture to check the preset and ask for any corrections.

c. Work Light Out

Most often the work light switch is on the stage manager's desk. He will handle the execution of this cue himself. It is possible that there may be house work lights on, too. The house electrician must be reminded to turn them out at this point.

d. House Lights Out (To house electrician)

The house electrician responds "HOUSE IS OUT," when he has accomplished this cue. This may be at some point before the completion of the overture. (The conductor will be lighted by the follow spot for the overture end.)

e. Stand By On Stage (To the beginning actors)

A final warning to the actors on stage that the curtain is about to rise.

f. Curtain Up

This may be cued at the end (or slightly before the end) of the applause for the overture.

g. Head High (To production electrician)

This is a cue for the electrician to bring up the front lights. It may be known as "Electrics Cue #1," or simply as "Head high." In any event, it is cued so that the front lights begin to come up when the curtain is about six feet off the deck. (Ergo, "Head high.")

N.B. 1: If an understudy announcement is to be made, it should be made between the time the house lights go to half and the orchestra starts the overture. This will make a new cue for the conductor to start the overture and must be pre-arranged with him. Also, if such an announcement is to be made, the sound man must be warned to have a "hot" mike for the stage manager.

N.B. 2: The lighting designer may have designed curtain warmers to operate during the overture. They will be cued (to the production electrician) at the beginning of the overture and cued out at the conclusion of the overture.

N.B. 3: Usually the only signal among the above which cannot be given verbally is the curtain signal. The curtain in many theatres operates from the fly floor or pin rail, and a signal light must be used for cuing purposes.

Standard operation of a light-cue system for the beginning or ending of an act is: Light ON—READY; Light OFF—Curtain UP (or DOWN). For curtain Calls: Light ON—Curtain UP; Light OFF—Curtain DOWN.

DURING THE ACT

1. Record the curtain time and all future times required by the time sheet.

2. Check lighting, including front lights.

3. Follow the performance pattern established during rehearsals and previous performances. This includes prompting, giving all warnings and cues, checking and double-checking actors' entrances, checking properties and warning the stage crews and orchestra that the end of the act is imminent.

It has been said that a good stage manager has a mysterious sixth sense, that during a performance he can spot trouble or errors intuitively. If the stage manager has integrated himself properly into the performance, there is nothing mysterious about his ability, and it is not an extra-sensory phenomenon. Any break in tempo, any foreign noise, any missing light or property, in other words, any break in performance pattern should register immediately on the stage manager's mind. In this vein, no stage manager should ever be at a loss to know when to ring a bell or when to lower a curtain. Just as an actor will know from the pattern that has been set when to interrupt another actor or when

102

to break into a pause, so will the stage manager know when to give his cues.

4. Signal the lowering of the curtain at the end of the act, and call for house lights after the audience has had an opportunity to applaud or react.

At the end of an act or scene, if a change of scenery is to be made, it is customary for all departments to await a signal from the stage manager before starting the change. This is necessary because the stage manager must determine that the curtain is completely down, and that actors have cleared the stage and are not in a position to be injured. Having determined these things, the stage manager gives the signal for the change. This may be done by calling the word "Strike!" Another method is for the stage manager to delay asking for work lights until he has determined that all is in readiness for the change. The appearance of the work lights would be the signal for all departments to start the change.

BETWEEN THE ACTS

1. The stage manager supervises the change of scenery and checks all details. It is customary for each department head to advise the stage manager that his own department is "set and ready."

2. An assistant calls the ensuing act and sees that the proper actors come to the stage. If the change is made easily and quickly, the call is made after the change. The actor should reach the stage in time to get prepared, but unnecessary waiting around should be avoided. If the change is complicated and takes the complete intermission, the assistant can time his call to the progress of the change. In this way he keeps the actors out of the way until the scenery is practically set and it is safe (literally) for the actor to come onstage. During this call the assistant can announce any special rehearsals that are being held the next day.

3. Ring the lobby signal in sufficient time to allow the audience to resume its seats.

4. Start the new act with the procedure adopted for the production.

5. Another example of performance pattern (or establishing good performance habits) may be added here. The performance check list

used by many stage managers often is inserted in the prompt script. The following has its humorous side, but it has happened far too often with disastrous results to be ignored. The stage manager, while checking onstage props, may put down his check list, which is in the prompt script, to adjust something, realize that time is short, rush offstage, ring up the curtain, and *then* discover that he has left the prompt script onstage! This can be avoided if the stage manager keeps his check list separate from his prompt script and never removes his script from his prompt desk where it belongs. Whatever method the stage manager sees fit to adopt, he must see that his habits are good ones, his performance pattern airtight.

The stage borrowed many of its methods and, consequently, its terms from the sea and from ships. "Good performance pattern" is a term that means the same thing as the borrowed term sometimes used about stage managers—"He knows how to *run his deck.*"

CURTAIN CALLS

Curtain calls show considerable variety. There are company calls, principal-actor calls, single calls, tableaux, and others. All of them must be treated as part of the performance pattern, and receive the same careful attention that other details of the performance receive.

One bit of technique in accomplishing curtain calls may be pointed out. The curtain, during the call, *apparently* stays open longer than it actually does. In practice, the stage manager gives the Curtain Up signal, then, when the curtain is several feet from its fully open position, he gives the Curtain Down signal. The time consumed by the stage hands stopping the upward movement of the curtain, overcoming inertia, and starting the curtain downward, allows the actors sufficient time to take their bows. An inexperienced stage manager may leave the curtain in its fully open position for several seconds before giving the Curtain Down signal. This results in an overlong curtain call, both for the actor and the audience.

AFTER THE FINAL CURTAIN

1. During the run of the play, no actor or understudy should leave the theater before the final curtain call unless permission has been

received from the stage manager. Permanent permission to leave early is given actors who have made their last onstage appearance before the play is over and are not required in the curtain calls. Their understudies also are given permission. It is accepted practice for all personnel who have such permission to check out with the stage manager as they leave. During rehearsals and tryout weeks, no actor should leave the theater until dismissed, even after the final curtain call, because notes may be given or rehearsals planned.

2. Remind the actors, understudies, and crew of any special rehearsals, or assignments for the following day. If the next performance is a matinee, an announcement to that effect should be made throughout the backstage area.

3. Enter the times in the diary, plus any pertinent information about the production; understudies on, cast members ill, rehearsals held during the day, etc. The *Stage Manager's Report* may be made out at this time.

4. Give notes to the technical staff or actors. If a prop or a piece of scenery has been damaged or broken during the performance, make sure that the proper person knows about it and that plans are being made to remedy the problem. If actors have press appointments, make sure they are reminded.

It is sometimes wise to give performance notes at this time. Sometimes it is unwise. Some actors are "up" after the performance and will not be paying strict attention. Some actors will have guests in their dressing rooms and full attention will be hard to get. Others will review the performance immediately after the show and can (indeed, should) be given notes at this time. The stage manager will have to use his judgment and his knowledge of the personalities of the company to guide him.

UNDERSTUDY REHEARSALS

The stage manager conducts understudy rehearsals. The acting pattern for rehearsals and for the performance has been established by the director while directing the original company. The understudy must fit himself into this pattern. Mimicking the actor who created the part is not wanted. But, insofar as the understudy is physically able, he must re-create the characterization evolved by the director and the actor who originated the part. This means that the understudy will copy physical action exactly. Readings and interpretations will not be changed except by the natural voice quality of the understudy. Additions such as "I have a little piece of business that would fit nicely here," or suggestions because the understudy "feels" that he "does this sort of thing rather well," or omissions because "I don't feel that cross," are not to be tolerated. If called upon to perform, the understudy must fit into the play as unobtrusively as possible.

When the understudies have been hired early in the rehearsal period, have attended all rehearsals and watched the direction, they will know what is expected of them. In a few instances, especially when the understudy also acts a part and cannot observe the actor he is understudying, it will be necessary for the stage manager to supply a great deal of information and direction. Even in this instance, the stage manager's job is to re-create direction, not to originate it.

The stage manager may encounter understudies, especially young and inexperienced ones, who feel that the above treatment is unnecessarily authoritarian. They will resent what they consider a limitation placed on their creative ability. There is a limitation, and the method is dictatorial. It must be. The stage manager should explain that this method is inherent in understudying and is not a special scheme of this particular producer. The method is essential for two reasons. First, the understudy will not rehearse with the actors, and so the actors will not be familiar with the understudy's possible deviations from the pattern. Second, the use of an understudy is an emergency matter, and, even if the actors were acquainted with the deviations, it would be too much to expect a company to adapt itself to these deviations on the spur of the moment. The understudy and actors usually have little or no warning before the understudy makes his appearance. It is not logical to expect fifteen actors to adapt themselves to one understudy in an emergency. It is logical to expect an understudy to prepare himself to fit into the group of fifteen.

106

It has been found that it is best to hold sufficient understudy rehearsals, so that each understudy can rehearse all of his parts completely at least once a week. These should be walking rehearsals, not line rehearsals. As soon as possible after the understudies are prepared, they should be given a full dress rehearsal complete with scenery, props, costumes, sound, and usually lighting.

Understudies, unlike the regular actors, rarely get an opportunity to solidify their performance before an audience in tryouts and dress rehearsals. Their work often never goes beyond the rehearsal stage. To help them prepare themselves to meet an audience, the stage manager should make provision for the understudies to watch performances. This will give them a before-an-audience point of view. Vicarious, to be sure, but useful.

COMPANY REHEARSALS

George M. Cohan is reputed to have said that periodic rehearsals of the company during the run of the play were necessary "to take out the improvements." When, weeks after the opening, one hears such remarks as, "The play seems so fresh that it is hard to realize that it has been running for months," or "I enjoyed this performance more than the opening night," the speakers are consciously or unconsciously paying the stage manager his finest compliment. It is after the opening and during the run of the play that the stage manager has his most difficult and arduous work. Keeping the production "fresh" is no easy matter.

The inanimate elements of the production, the scenery, costumes, lights, and properties, are obviously in first-class condition or they are not. Keeping them in condition may require a certain amount of time, patience, and ingenuity, but determining their condition should present no problem. Moreover, the stage manager has highly trained production crew heads at his command to accomplish any repairs and replacements necessary to keep this section of the production fresh.

On the other hand, it is the duty of the stage manager, with only occasional assistance from the director, to see that the actors keep their part of the production fresh. This is especially true during a tour, when the production is removed from the aegis of the producer and director.

107

An actor's primary means of expression is his emotions. In his characterization his basic thinking is done for him by the playwright. This is not meant to imply that there are not fine minds among actors. But for characterization purposes their thinking pattern is established for them by the playwright. During the rehearsal period, the actor, with the director's help, experiments and elaborates within this thinking pattern and evolves a complete characterization, which he conveys to the audience by his emotions. Consequently, by nature or choice, or because of the demands of his profession, the actor's emotions are constantly alerted and receptive to suggestion. It is to be expected that he will consciously or unconsciously receive suggestions and incorporate them into his characterization. It is the stage manager's responsibility, after the opening performance, to screen these additions.

When the playwright, director, and producer are completely satisfied with a performance, one often hears: "Freeze that—keep the show exactly like that." In a general way this is a sound admonition. But, like all generalities, it has qualifications. First, in the legitimate theater it is not possible to "freeze" all elements of a production. An obvious example is the audience. No two audiences are exactly alike because of numerous reasons, and certainly an actor's performance must adjust to the audience. Second, it is not in the nature of things to remain static. Change is far more natural. It is with these two qualifications that the stage manager is concerned.

There is little any stage manager can do about the first qualification except to keep alert to it and help the actor adjust to it. The second qualification calls for constant vigilance and is the outstanding element of the production that must be under the control of the stage manager at all times.

The majority of changes considered by the actor will be thought to be for the betterment of his characterization and, consequently, of the play. Whether they are or not the stage manager must decide. No conscious change should be made by an actor without a consultation with the stage manager, and no change of any considerable size or consequence may be made without consultation with the director. The limits of the actor's ability and his mind (they are not necessarily alike) will often guide the stage manager in his decision. If a generalization may be made at all, it might be said that a change should meet this requirement; when one first meets the change, does it immediately appear evident that the play needs the change for its own good? If it does, fine; if it does not, it generally may be discarded.

It has been presumed changes are made consciously. This is not true always. In fact, most changes are made unconsciously and intuitively. These changes are often small and may be exceedingly insidious. The stage manager must be constantly alert to them and, if they are harmful, stop them. The new change will be hard to get rid of, once it has become established.

It has been presumed, also, the stage manager has personal integrity, experience, and discernment, and is capable of sitting in judgment on changes. Should a discussion of a change be unresolved, the problem must be referred to the director and producer.

The stage manager has no more exhilarating experience in the theater than watching and being a partner in the continuing development of a good actor's characterization during the run of the play. The subtle changes that indicate a growth of understanding, meaning, and feeling are fascinating to observe and must be nurtured by patience and understanding. Much time and thought will be expended, but the experience itself is reward enough.

There is probably no more exasperating experience than to watch an inept actor, no matter how well-meaning, tamper with the characterization the playwright and director have created for him. He will be the actor requiring most thorough and tactful controlling.

It is in the nature of things that a percentage of human beings are equipped with an overabundance of prankishness or irresponsibility or just plain cussedness. Such stupidities as self-aggrandizement or "scene-stealing" at the expense of the play are not to be tolerated. When the stage manager has ascertained that a change has been made by an actor prompted by the above unwanted motives, the actor should be brought back into line promptly and without ceremony, just as such people are in any well-ordered society.

And so, when need there be a company rehearsal? The answer is, rarely, if the stage manager has been conscientious in his duties. Usually only after notes and discussions fail to get results. The athletic team that does not respond to talks and lectures is taken to the field and made to *do* it. So it is with an acting company.

A considerable part of the stage manager's job of keeping the company fresh is keeping himself fresh. A resume of the stage manager's progress to this point may help the reader understand how this is done.

Beginning as a manuscript and ending as a finished production before an audience, the play has progressed through several periods, the writing, the planning and rehearsing, the polishing, the performing. The stage manager advances with the play through these periods. The technical progress of the play and the part the stage manager has in that section of the production should be obvious by now and will not be repeated. However, it will be advantageous to review briefly the nontechnical progress of the stage manager, the over-all development of his integration into the play.

The stage manager's first important period of development and integration is during the rehearsals. By watching the director and actors develop characterizations, by being thoroughly familiar with stage business, by "sharing" the emotions of the actor, by knowing the rhythms and tempos of the performance, by being in rapport with the actor, the stage manager will grow into the play along with the actor.

During the polishing period (the run-through, dress rehearsal, and tryout periods), the stage manager will combine what he has acquired in rehearsals with the technical elements of the production and solidify his part in the performance pattern. He is now an integral part of the production, of each performance.

The stage manager stays in the performance pattern until after the New York opening and until after everyone is comfortably set in the pattern, and then he breaks free from it. Usually this is not done abruptly but over a period of several performances, during which time his assistants take over his technical part in the pattern. If the stage

110

manager is to advance into the next period of progress, this break must be made and it must be complete.

A stage manager who does not divorce himself from the performance pattern often lands in the pitfall that besets the actor, because he will respond to the same emotional stimuli that the actor does. It has been seen that many changes in the actor's performance are intuitive, small, and insidious. If the stage manager is in the performance pattern, he will be drawn along in the same emotional stream that influences the actor and will make the same intuitive errors the actor makes. However, if he is outside the pattern, outside the influence of the stream, he can approach the period of managing the run of the play.

There will be times when he re-enters the pattern to resume his onstage duties. He re-enters the pattern in a different way when he watches a performance from the audience. The ability to shift from the subjective to objective is a quality the stage manager must have either naturally or by training, or he will be unable to manage the long-running play. Remaining in the subjective, in the performance pattern, is emotionally exhausting, and the stage manager's duties may turn into mechanical chores. If the stage manager can become objective in his approach to the production, he will not exhaust himself and will have strength to meet the job of managing the long run, a job which will become an increasingly exciting challenge.

In these few preceding pages an attempt has been made to emphasize the qualification the producer is most likely to look for in his stage manager, the ability to keep the show fresh. To be sure, the skilled workman must know his tools. Experience in summer theaters, college theaters, and other places can furnish much of the mechanics of stage managing. This handbook will help in that direction. However, with but isolated exceptions, there is no place except Broadway or a long road tour in which the stage manager is required to do his most difficult work, manage the long run. Unless a stage manager is capable of sustaining opening-night freshness, even great skill in mechanics will not save him from the epithet "button-pusher and callboy." Only the man capable of handling this important duty may be truly called a stage manager.

111

REPLACEMENTS IN THE ACTING COMPANY

Occasionally actors withdraw from a company that has been running some time and will probably continue its run. A replacement must be found. Normally the producer, director, and playwright select the replacement, but sometimes the stage manager is given the job. As much thought and care should go into the selection of a replacement as into the original casting. Reference to the alternates on the original Cast List (see page 31) should be helpful. Also the advantage of having kept the actors file up-to-date should be obvious.

If the replacement is a star or featured actor in the New York company, the director usually handles the rehearsals. The stage manager often conducts rehearsals for small-part replacements. On the road the stage manager usually rehearses all replacements.

The stage manager will be guided by the director's original direction and the pattern that has been established. Stage business and the general characterization should not be altered. Minor changes due to fundamental personality differences between the original actor and the replacement must be expected. Also, as the replacement will rehearse with the regular members of the company, a greater latitude may be given the replacement than the understudy, especially if the replacement is a star. However, the stage manager's primary aim is to install the replacement with ease and comfort and as unobtrusively as possible.

The stage manager sometimes works alone with the replacement or utilizes understudies during the early rehearsals, when establishing stage business is the primary goal. However, when work on characterization starts, the actual company must be used. Obviously, understudies will not be used for rehearsals involving a star or featured player replacement unless the star so requests, although private rehearsals with the stage manager are useful timesavers. Likewise, one cannot expect to use the acting company during all rehearsals of a very minor character. Nevertheless, all replacements have a right to a full dress rehearsal with the acting company before their first public performance.

112

1. Has all vital show information been entered in the diary?
2. Has the Payroll Memorandum been given to the company manager?
3. Is the address list up to date?
4. Are the Stage Manager's Reports prepared and submitted?
5. Have the weekly bills of the department crew heads been checked, OK'd, and handed on to the company manager? The company manager will determine day to be submitted.
6. Are the understudies completely prepared?
7. Is the acting company in good shape? Have you watched each scene *from the audience* at least once this week?
8. How are the scenery, lights, props, costumes, sound? Fresh? In good repair?
9. Have you and your assistants shifted jobs recently, so that each assistant may see the show from the audience?
10. Have you a list of actors available as replacements in case of emergencies? (If flu of epidemic proportions hits your company, what happens if you run out of understudies?)
11. Have you filed all accident reports, whether or not the services of a doctor were required? (Forms are furnished by manager.)
12. Do you know how to obtain the services of the house physician quickly?
13. Have you caught up on the sleep you lost during rehearsals?

PART FIVE

Touring

This Part supplements sections on the out-of-town
tryout and the setup in Part Three and applies
chiefly to the long road tour.

PREPARATION FOR THE TOUR

I. Simplifying the Physical Production. During the New York run the
stage manager will be planning simplifications of the physical
production for the road tour. The acting company usually remains as it
is in New York, but very often a large number of the physical elements
of the production can be eliminated or simplified. The changes will be
more in the nature of streamlining than complete amputations.
Production values must be retained. A traveler on his first trip often
takes many more things than he needs. His second trip will see his
luggage reduced. It is a similar attitude toward trimming production
elements that governs the production staff. In an effort to insure the
success of his new play, the producer may overload the New York
company with extra or overelaborate production elements. Many of
these elements will be found to have no essential production value and,
although they are retained in New York because they are there, may be
removed for a touring show.

The stage manager and production crew heads instigate most
suggestions for simplification as their on-the-spot contact with the
production offers them the greatest opportunity to discover them. As
the line between elements that enrich a production rather than overload
it is very fine, their suggestions are submitted to the producer, director,
and designer for discussion and approval well in advance of the date of
the projected tour.

II. Timesavers. The term "short cut" has been avoided because it
connotes slipshod or skimpy methods and practices. However, short
cuts that save time without in any way reducing efficiency or depriving
the show of its full production values should be discovered and utilized.

Alert production crew heads will have suggestions, particularly for the setup period. The stage manager should find others. Many timesavers can be planned and prepared before the tour starts. Others will be discovered as the tour progresses.

Methods of lighting the show quickly are useful, because often too much is expended needlessly on this production element. The physical nature of the setup will determine, in part, the stage manager's method, but the lighting will be an accurate reproduction of the original.

Sometimes it is considered necessary for the scenery to be set and work lights put out before lighting can start. During the original lighting of the show that was true, but now the stage manager is reproducing the lighting, not creating it. If he must wait for the scenery, much time is wasted; and, once he does start, the other departments cannot work, because there is no light! Any scheme or short cut for overlapping activity without hurting the production will be a valuable timesaver.

A play composed of interior settings will depend on the equipment on the first pipe for most of its lighting. If the following preparations are made after the original lighting has been completed, most of the instruments can be focused at the next setup, while they are being mounted on the pipe, which will be near the floor for easy access.

1. Get exact height of pipe from floor when in position.
2. Make permanent arrangements, so that relation of pipe to portal is always the same.
3. Mark on the pipe the exact position of each instrument's hanger or clamp.
4. Mark each instrument as follows:
   a. Number of position on pipe
   b. Alignment marks on clamp and arm to set stage L. or R. direction
   c. Alignment marks on instrument and hanger arm or yoke to set tilt of instrument
   d. Mark focus.

If all instruments are in their proper places on the pipe when mounted by men working at floor level and individual alignment marks are correct, then they should be in position when the pipe is raised and properly adjusted to the portal. Only minor adjustments, if any, will be needed. Moreover, this focusing can be done while full work lights are on, while other departments are using most of the stage, and before, during, or after the scenery (except the portal, which is usually the first thing up anyway) is set up.

The above method of saving time should not be construed as being the best or only possible scheme. It is a sample, that's all. However, this type of short cut eliminates nothing but time and is valuable. All departments should be scrutinized for such possible timesavers. Short cuts that eliminate lighting instruments, scenery, properties, costumes, and, consequently, production values should not be resorted to except in emergency and then should be in the nature of planned emergency simplification.

III. Emergency Simplification. Emergencies arise in spite of the most careful planning and preparation for a tour. After the advance agent has checked the stage and delivered the hanging plot and other advices, the stage house may be altered structurally, and no one bother to tell the touring company before it arrives. Hemp lines may be old, but no one has taken the trouble to check them. Traps may be cut incorrectly. Movie sound horns and screens should have been removed, but are not. Also delayed trains cause late arrival in a town, and valuable time is lost. Methods of eliminating valuable elements in the physical production should be considered for such emergencies. The stage manager and production crew heads will discuss what emergency steps can be taken and will plan their execution.

Time saved by simplification of the setup may prevent cancellation or delayed start of a performance. Time saved in the taking down and loading out may prevent missing a train. Eliminating platforms, staircases, cornices, baseboards, wainscoting, backings, and ceilings may be considered in the scenery department. Eliminating a single piece of furniture will save time, if one realizes the time it takes to remove it from the baggage car, unpack it from its crate, unwrap it from its padded covers, and then, after the performance, to repad it, recrate it, and reload it into the baggage car. Most eliminations will come in the carpentry and property departments, as eliminations in the other departments bring too many complications. Leaving out a few lighting instruments might mean such a complete new switchboard hookup th.tt the time consumed plotting and understanding the new hookup would be greater than the time saved by not hanging the instruments. Generally sound effects cannot be eliminated, nor can costumes.

After being determined, these emergency simplifications should be discussed with the actors so that they are familiar with the changes that will be made in the performance pattern. Very often elimination of a physical element of the production brings dialogue and stage business changes.

No emergency simplification should be resorted to for any reason other than the planned one. Reducing the production because of "convenience" or laziness should not be permitted. Podunk must see as complete a physical production as Broadway, all things being equal.

IV. Preparing the Acting Company Many actors have had touring experience, but there may be some in the company who have not. The stage manager will advise them of what they may expect and what is required of them.

A. THE CALL. The material found in Part Three of this handbook should be brought to the attention of the company.

B. TRAVELING. Although the crew, the stage manager, and others may "travel ahead," *all actors travel with the company at all times.* The producer is the only one who may make an exception to this rule.

C. HOTELS. The discussion on hotel reservations in Part Three should be reviewed.

D. TRUNKS. In addition to the information in Part Three, the company should know that during one-night stands hotel trunks are not delivered daily but are left in the baggage car, if the same car will be used for the next move, or are stored during the day by the transfer company. However, hotel trunks must be *available* to the actors *at least once every week,* even during one-night stands. This is usually accomplished on the day when a theater with an unusually large stage is to be played. The hotel trunks are brought to the theater, not delivered to hotels, because some actors may not have a hotel reservation for that one day. The trunks are put in an out-of-the-way place where the actors will have access to them without disrupting the production. Theater trunks must be brought to the theater daily.

E. HAND LUGGAGE. Hand luggage is the individual's personal responsibility, and he will be expected to handle it as he sees fit. Personnel inexperienced in touring should be advised that they will be wise to keep hand luggage to a minimum. Today trains are crowded, and red-caps and taxis scarce. This is especially true on Sundays and at late hours, the normal traveling day and time for a touring company.

F. REHEARSALS. The actors should realize that regular understudy and any necessary company rehearsals will be held during the tour just as they are in New York.

G. SICKNESS. It is even more important that the management be kept advised of the health of the actor while he is on tour than when he is in New York.

H. SIMPLIFICATIONS AND EMERGENCIES. The stage manager will discuss and rehearse with the actors all planned emergency simplifications that he and the crew heads have decided upon. This may mean cutting or transposing dialogue, rearranging stage business and so on.

ON ARRIVAL AT THE NEW STAND

The stage manager will inspect the theater as soon as he can. He is the one who will decide what emergency or other simplification is necessary, if any.

There are many small things the stage manager can do to smooth out the arrival of the rest of the company, when he is traveling ahead with the crew.

He can check hotel reservations to see that they are being held. This is particularly important if the company is arriving by a late train and may mean that more desirable rooms are held.

He can check the position and spelling of names on the theater marquee. Errors can be corrected before the actors see them.

He can confirm appointments with newspaper or radio people. It has happened that stage managers have filled in on a radio program when the company is delayed, rather than lose valuable air time.

There may be other things he will do. However, his first duty is at the theater, seeing that the setup is under way and progressing satisfactorily.

LOADING IN, OR THE NEW SETUP

The following terms mean:

Load (or Take) In—Transferring the production from the baggage cars or from a storehouse or just from a truck and putting it into the theater

Set Up—Assembling the production in the theater for a performance

Take Down—Dismantling the production and preparing it for transportation

Load (or Put) Out—Transferring the production from the theater and into the baggage cars

However, as loading in and setting up are almost continuous or simultaneous operations at most touring stands, the terms are used interchangeably. Likewise with taking down and loading out.

There are times when all four terms are applicable. E.g., over a week end the production may be loaded in on Sunday with the setup on Monday. The following Saturday night the production might be taken down, and then on Sunday it would be loaded out.

The stage manager will be at the theater at the appointed hour for the call and will be in attendance throughout the setup. His duties include:

I. Dressing Rooms. He will assign and personally check all dressing rooms, toilets, and other facilities. He will check that trunks and costumes are properly distributed. The posted dressing room list should include a reminder of matinee days, and half-hour and curtain times, all of which may change from city to city.

II. Answering Questions. No two stage houses are alike, and so problems will arise. He will answer questions and make decisions.

120

III. Prompt Desk. He will place the prompt desk and check all cuing devices, including fixed equipment belonging to the theater. He will establish with the house electrician a half-mark for the house lights and the routine used for opening and closing each act.

IV. Lighting. He will light the show quickly and accurately.

V. Curtains. Because of its weight or rigging, the house curtain may be easy or difficult to operate, slow or fast. With the actual men who will operate the curtain during the performance, the stage manager will test and rehearse the speed of the curtain. Some people's reaction time is slower than others. This rehearsal gives the stage manager an opportunity to time the curtains exactly. The curtain men should be advised of the number of curtain calls normally taken and when they are taken. Usually curtain calls come after the final act, but in some productions, especially revivals of stylized plays, there are curtain calls after other acts.

VI. Interviewing and Rehearsing Extras. After the stage manager has experienced two or three moves and their consequent setups, he should have a fairly accurate time schedule established. He will arrange that the call for interviewing extras and the time allotted for their costuming and rehearsing do not interfere with other departments. Very often the rehearsal can be accomplished during the stage crew run-through.

VII. Stage Crew Run-through. A run-through for the technical departments will be held, if advisable. Normally, a technical rehearsal with the actors present is not necessary.

VIII. Time Sheet. The stage manager will supply the house crew heads with the running time of the show, by acts and scenes. He will warn them of quiet scenes and other production specialties to be alert to.

IX. Orchestra. He will meet with the orchestra leader and discuss music and cuing.

X. Performance Pattern. He will take notes on any variation to the performance pattern and will advise all personnel concerned.

XI. Acoustics. Test the acoustics of the theater for voices. Test theater-furnished PA systems, especially if used in conjunction with production-furnished electronic sound equipment.

121

I. Keeping in Touch. Keep the New York production office advised concerning the show via time sheets or other methods.

II. Address List. Be sure that the company manager and all assistant stage managers have a copy of the new address list for each city. If the address list is combined with the personnel check-off list, be sure the above people know who is traveling ahead and who is traveling with the company.

It is good practice to post on the call board of each stand the local addresses and phone numbers of the company manager and all stage managers.

III. Hotels. Keep hotel information for future stands available for all. Sometimes the advance agent deals directly with the stage manager in matters pertaining to hotel reservations. Other times he relays the information through the company manager. In any event the actors will look to the stage manager for advice about hotels, and he will do all he can to assist them.

IV. Trunks. Prepare a new hotel trunk pickup list for this stand and a delivery list for the next stand.

V. Rehearsals. The stage manager will find out local rules governing understudy and/or company rehearsals on the stage, the use of lights, props, and other facilities. Managing to find time for understudy rehearsals during a tour is always a problem, but they must not be neglected. A wise stage manager defers to the understudies if a time most congenial to the majority is suggested.

VI. Anticipating Change in Performance Pattern. The stage manager will anticipate changes in the performance pattern for the next stand. E.g., the Erlanger in Buffalo has a very peculiarly shaped and crowded Offstage Right area. Further complications arise, because all entrances from the dressing rooms to the stage are made through a door in the Downstage Rightstage wall. Knowing these things in advance will help the stage manager plan necessary performance pattern changes.

Problems will be presented not only by small stages but by overlarge stages (Des Moines), unique dressing room arrangements (Forrest,

122

Philadelphia), flooring downstage laid on concrete, traps impossible (Kansas City), and so on.

The problems to be met at well-known theaters can be solved weeks in advance. The advance agent will keep the company posted on stage conditions. Further advice may be received from the production crew heads and from actors who have made recent tours.

If necessary, rehearsals of performance pattern changes should be held at a previous stand while there is leisure time, rather than waiting until the new stand's setup day.

VII. Actors' File. It has happened that emergencies in the acting company arise for which the planned understudy coverage (even double-cover) is not sufficient. Most stage managers keep a personal file of actors for such contingencies. The New York office will have replacement actors in mind; but, when you are in St. Paul, New York is pretty far away.

This personal actors' file often is composed of actors the stage manager knows who live in the area where the show is playing or actors he has met during the tour. While playing large cities, the stage manager frequently is visited by actors seeking employment. If they seem likely prospects, the stage manager can sound them out for willingness to act temporarily in such an emergency. Quite obviously these actors can be used in small parts only and must be good studies. If the emergency occurs in St. Paul or Des Moines or Omaha, a call to Chicago can produce an actor in a couple of hours, whereas a New York replacement might not arrive in time to prevent cancellation of a performance.

Most cities large enough to support a road show will have very capable radio, television, or university and little-theater actors available for such emergencies.

It must be understood that the situation described is an *extreme* emergency, one that threatens to close the show. No production, touring or otherwise, should be running without competent and complete understudy coverage.

VIII. Cooperation. Touring is a cooperative venture for all concerned, particularly for the company and stage managers. The actual mechanics of moving from city to city, the business end of the theater, are in the provinces of the company manager and the advance agent. However, in his role of liaison staff member, the stage manager will work in close association with the front of the house and will be called upon to assist and give advice in many problems. The stage manager is in the best position to know the interests, the community pulse, of backstage personnel, and so he will be expected to make suggestions for their welfare. To make suggestions intelligently, it behooves the stage manager to have a knowledge of the duties and problems that face the company manager and the advance agent. From suggesting train times to counting up, if the company manager is ill; from relaying information about appointments to filling in when an actor cannot get to an appointment, will be problems that may face the stage manager.

When the stage manager travels ahead, he and the company manager exchange some of their duties. The stage manager may help the company manager by doing certain routine front-of-the-house matters before the company manager arrives. While the stage manager is ahead of the others, the company manager helps the assistant stage managers with company problems that may arise.

The dividing line between the front of the house and backstage is very faint in a touring company. The closer the relationship between stage manager and company manager, the more efficiently the tour will be conducted, and company morale will be higher.

LOADING OUT

I. Schedule. After the final performance the stage manager usually stays in attendance during the taking down and loading out of the production. He will check that:

    a. Dismantling and loading is on schedule

    b. All parts of the production are removed from the theater

    c. Dressing rooms have been cleared of theater trunks, wardrobe, make-up, and any personal property of the company

II. The Call. He will see that the Call is picked up by the carpenter or himself.

III. Traveling Ahead. It is not unusual for the stage crew to travel to the next city on a train many hours ahead of that taken by the acting company. In fact, the setup in the new city may be under way before the company leaves the last stand. The stage manager will want to be at the new theater when the new setup starts, and so he will travel with the crew. Traveling ahead (which includes loading out, the actual trip, and the new setup) is very fatiguing work for a stage manager, because he loses meals and sleep and does not get the few respites that the stage hands do during a performance. The stage manager should train his assistants, so that traveling ahead can be alternated among the stage-managing staff. Generally the stage manager sends an assistant ahead when the theater at the next stand presents no problem or change in performance pattern.

KEEPING THE COMPANY FRESH

Just one thing can be added to what has been written about keeping the company fresh, and that is more of an extension to "Company Rehearsals" in Part Four than a distinct addition.

During the run of the play in New York, many of the personnel will have little more to do with each other outside the theater, outside business hours as it were, than the average office worker will have with his fellow workers. When the performance is over, the individuals will separate and return to their respective families and friends. This is natural since New York is the permanent home of many actors, and the paths of fellow workers need not cross. On tour the company will be thrown together almost continuously. Long train trips, living in the same hotels, eating at the same restaurants, separation from friends, few opportunities to make new acquaintances are among the factors that bring personnel together intimately. A sort of traveling community is created.

An actor's performance will be influenced by his daily life—that should be obvious. As the stage manager is responsible for performances, he should do all in his power to make the touring-company community a happy one. Many members of the company will take advantage of each new city's parks, beaches,

125

museums, and other points of interest. They will attend concerts and movies and sporting events. They will seek out things to do to substitute for their normal home activities. The stage manager must be alert to the personnel's extracurricular activities, as they should influence his planning of company or understudy rehearsals and other company activities.

No blanket statement can be made as to where the stage manager's solicitude for personnel should start or end. The character of the personnel in a particular company will help the stage manager determine this for himself. One point, however, should be mentioned. The producer, by signing an Equity contract with the actor, acquires exclusive right to the actor's services. Any outside employment and, as an extension of this, any outside activity that has a deleterious effect on an actor's performance will be of vital interest to the producer and, consequently, the stage manager. The producer presumes the stage manager will concern himself with an actor's outside activity in so far as the welfare of the production is affected.

CANADIAN TOURS

Extended Canadian tours are rare, but shows that include Buffalo in their itinerary often include Toronto. The manifests, bonds, and arrangements necessary to enter and leave Canada are the company manager's headache, but there are two things the stage manager will supervise.

1. Obtain a set of keys from each actor for each of his trunks, hotel and theater. Tag these keys for identification purposes and turn them over to the property man. When the company enters Canada, trunks will be examined by Canadian Customs *in the baggage car,* with usually no one but the property man in attendance. A wise actor will retain a duplicate set of keys.

2. When the company leaves Canada to return to the States, the American Customs will furnish a representative, who will be in attendance at the theater during the last performance and during the taking-down and loading-out period. During the performance he will assist the actors and other personnel in preparing their individual

126

customs declarations. The stage manager can assist by routing actors to this representative when they have leisure time. During the loading-out period, the customs man will examine all actors' theater trunks, all wardrobe department trunks, hampers, prop boxes, etc., etc., before they are closed, will supervise locking them, and will affix a seal. Hotel trunks, which will have been picked up previously, will have been examined before the last performance in the presence of the property man, and will have been sealed into the baggage car.

If there are alien actors in the company, the company manager will handle the details of clearing them for entrance to and return from Canada *with the company and at the proper time*. The stage manager must impress on these aliens that care should be taken when playing border cities. A sight-seeing tour of Niagara Falls with a short visit across the International Bridge just "to see the view" can turn into a prolonged stay as a guest of Immigrations!.

STAGE MANAGER'S EQUIPMENT

During the tour the stage manager will need a certain amount of equipment and supplies. It can be seen that he is constantly preparing new trunk, dressing room, and other lists. A typewriter is practically indispensable. Also, he will need, in varying degrees of importance and frequency, paper, carbons, thumbtacks, scotch tape, pencils, erasers, a supply of time sheets, extra manuscripts, extra parts, chalk, envelopes, stamps, clipboards, scratch pads, pencil sharpeners, scissors, ruler, tape, paper clips, paper fasteners, a stapler, ink, colored pencils, first-aid kit. Ingenious work boxes have been devised to accommodate these supplies. On the other hand, they can be wrapped in an old newspaper and tucked away in an empty corner of a property or lighting crate. In a small production having practically no cues, a stage manager can get along with almost nothing, not even the traditional music stand to hold his prompt script. In a heavy production, the stage manager usually has equipment of his choice carried with the production to guarantee adequate and standard prompt-desk facilities. In this matter, as in all others, the stage manager will choose his own method of how to accomplish his duties.

127

Eventually the show closes, either temporarily or permanently. If the closing is temporary, the producer will store the production intact or practically so. Preparing the production for storage is a cooperative task for the production crew heads, the company manager, and the stage manager, based on directives from the producer.

I. Temporary Closing. Lighting and sound equipment is usually rented. It is returned to the owner after complete lists and special notes have been made, so that the equipment can be reassembled or replaced exactly. The scenery, props, and costumes are inventoried, packed, and stored as directed by the producer.

Packing is handled by the production crew heads, who take precautions against damage by the elements, bad handling, moths, etc.

Inventories and lists are compiled by the production crew heads, prepared in at least triplicate by the stage manager (he has the typewriter!), collected and organized by the company manager, and then turned over to the producer.

All containers—crates, boxes, trunks, bundles—are numbered and labeled, and a master list is compiled as a record. Each container has its individual label and packing lists, one list inside the container and the other affixed to the outside. The third copy of the list is collected, with the inventories, for the producer, and a notation of the place of storage is made on it. These inventories and packing lists give the producer exact knowledge of the whereabouts of any and all production elements.

The remainder of the production—personnel, manuscripts, stationery, time sheets, and personal trunks—is brought to New York City. Trunks are delivered as requested; the rule for delivering in New York City is the same as that for collecting. (See Part Three.) Manuscripts, etc. are collected by the stage manager and delivered to the producer. A final address list of all personnel is compiled.

II. Closing Permanently. When a show closes on the road, lighting and sound equipment, personnel and personal trunks, manuscripts and time sheets will be brought to New York City as they are for a temporary closing. Scenery, props, and costumes are disposed of locally, *in toto* if possible, in order to save the cost of handling and transporting to another city.

The producer usually gives considerable thought to the disposal of his production, unless the closing is sudden and unexpected. He has several alternatives—selling, giving away, destroying, or storing.

Scenery, the most valuable element, is the most difficult to sell. It is usually given away or destroyed, almost never stored. The local house carpenter may take it as a gift in order to salvage valuable stage hardware and lumber. Little theaters and other organizations sometimes will accept it but rarely have funds for paying for it. A great deal of scenery is taken to the local dump and destroyed.

Small properties of slight value are given to the taker, often the house property man. Those not taken are destroyed. Good pieces of furniture and carpeting can usually be sold for enough to warrant their transportation to New York City.

Modern costumes, especially street clothes, are sometimes bought by the actors who wear them. Secondhand clothing dealers will buy some things. Welfare or charitable organizations will welcome the opportunity to collect serviceable clothing and furniture. Period costumes are bought by costume-rental houses or may be given to little theaters, schools or to organizations that can salvage the material in them. Wardrobe baskets and trunks, well-made property boxes and crates are brought to New York and stored for use by a future production.

By careful planning, company managers and stage managers can dispose of all elements of the production profitably, either by selling them or by giving them into the hands of a deserving organization or individual.

129

APPENDIXES

Appendix A:
The Manuscript as Received from
the Playwright

                          John
Whenever I find that the . . .

                    (The telephone rings)

                          Daisy
                    (Picking up the phone on her desk)
John Smithers' office. Miss Caramel speaking.

                    (Hanson's angry voice is heard over the
                    phone, but the words are not distin-
                    guishable. Daisy holds the receiver
                    away from her ear, and each time Hanson
                    pauses for a breath Daisy tries to
                    speak.)

Yes, Mr. Han . . .

                    (Hanson has a fresh breath and goes
                    on talking for quite a while.)

But, if you'd just let me . . .

                    (Again Hanson speaks)

                    (John has been quietly amused with
                    Daisy's predicament and decides to
                    offer his help. He takes the phone
                    from Daisy and shouts into it.)

                          John
                    (Shouting)
Listen, you old bag of wind, settle down!

                    (Hanson continues angrily but soon quiets
                    down, and the audience no longer can
                    hear him.)

                          John (con't)
Fine! Fine! I'll see you tonight about eight-thirty.
                    (He hands the phone back to Daisy, who
                    replaces the receiver in its cradle.)
Hanson can drown out a brass band when he gets started. Hard on the
ears . . .
                    (then, slyly)
          . . . especially such pretty pink ones, like yours.

                    (Daisy is embarrassed and, to tell
                    the truth, a bit apprehensive.)

                          Daisy
Oh, Mister Smithers!

                    John
          (Resuming his office manner)
Yes, yes, ah . . . well, yes. I think we have time for one more letter.

                    Daisy
          (With regained aplomb.)
Certainly, Mr. Smithers.

                    John
          (Dictating)
"Mr. A. Brush Wallaby"
          (aside to Daisy)
Put this on my personal stationery. You'll find his address in my
personal address book under Australia.
          (dictating again)
"Dear Wally" comma "Long time no hear from" dash "anxious to hear how
things progress with all the supalia" period. That's . . .
          (He spells it out)
. . . s - u - p - a - l - i - a . . .
          (Explaining, a bit self-consciously)
you know, plural diminutive for marsupial. Ha, ha! Well, ahem, ah ...
          (Resumes his dictation)
"Molly and the kids pester the life out of me asking me when . . ."

               (The telephone rings again and
               Daisy answers it.)

                    Daisy
          (into telephone)
John Smithers' office, Miss Caramel speaking.
          (She listens for a moment)
Why, yes, Mr. Filibuster.

               (John is startled. He gesticulates wildly
               that he is "not in", that he has "gone out".
               At first Daisy apparently does not under-
               stand, and so, while she continues to
               listen to the phone, John re-enacts that he
               is "not in". We know that Daisy is just
               playing a game and are not surprised when
               she nods her head that she understands.
               John heaves a big sigh of relief, gets his
               hat from the closet, and starts out. As
               he passes Daisy he pats her on the shoulder.)

               (Daisy is left alone on the stage listening
               to Mr. Filibuster on the phone as

               The Curtain descends very, very slowly.)

1-4-38

ACT ONE, Scene 4

(It is shortly after eight o'clock the
evening of the same day and we find our-
selves in Harry Hanson's house, in his
own workroom and hideaway, to be exact.
This is a small but comfortable room
with well-worn chairs and with shelves
for many books. A small table-desk is
at one side, a fireplace in the wall
opposite, a door leads to the rest of
the house. Through the darkened windows
we see vivid flashes of lightning, and
the thunder fairly shakes the house.
When the curtain rises we see Harry
sitting before the flickering fire reading the evening paper. Voices are
heard from offstage, and Harry putting
aside his paper, rises as Tom Albion
and Dick Bestor enter.)

Harry

Glad to see you could make it tonight, Tom.

(They shake hands)

Tom

You know I never miss these sessions, Harry.

Harry
(To Dick Bestor)
Richard Bestor, my old college roommate and lifelong pal. Richard
Bestor. How are you, Dick?

Dick

Fine, Harry, just fine.

(They shake hands)

Harry

Make yourselves comfortable. John should be along any minute now. I
talked to him on the phone this afternoon - said he'd try to get here
by eight-thirty.

(There is a bright flash of lightning,
followed by a tremendous clap of
thunder.)

Hope this storm doesn't keep him away.

Dick

He hates driving in the rain.

Tom

I don't know that I blame him. That hill down from his house is really
treacherous during a storm.

Dick

We had a bad scare on it the other day when I was driving back from the
Canajoharie Country Club.

Harry

How did you get onto that road? We always use the Tallahassee-Spokane
Highway coming from the Club.

Dick

Bill Crunch's wife had their car and we were taking him home. It wouldn't
have been . . .

(The telephone rings)

Harry
(answering)

Yes?
(He listens)
Oh, hello, Molly . . .

(Voices are heard offstage)

Just a second, Molly . . .
(He listens to the voices)
You don't have to worry, he just arrived.

(John enters)

Harry (con't)
(into phone)

One minute and I'll put him on.
(Hands phone to John)
It's Molly, John.

John
(into phone)

Hello, dear.
(He listens)
Now just relax and take it easy - I'll be OK.
(Listens. Harry signals him that he
would like to say something to Molly.)
Certainly, dear, certainly. Harry wants to talk to you again.
(Passes phone to Harry)

                    Harry
             (into phone)
Molly, now don't you worry. This storm will be over in a halfhour . . .

             (Terrific lightning and thunder)

. . . at least I think it will be. Everything's under control. Yes . . .
yes . . . Right! Goodbye.
             (He hangs up)

                    John
Molly gets into quite a state on nights like this if I'm out in it.
Spends most of her time on the phone calling the neighbors.

                    Tom
Don't blame her. Dick was just telling us he had a bad time on that hill
of yours the other day.

                    Dick
Fortunately we were just creeping along. Even so we turned completely
around. Nothing else in sight and stayed on the road. Lucky. Glad I'm
within walking distance tonight. You too, eh, Tom?

                    Tom

You bet!

                    John
Yes, Molly worries and hangs onto the phone - does all day, anyway, storm
or no storm.

                    Harry
             (Who has been trying the radio,
              abandons it)
Nothing but static. Drink, John?
             (He starts to mix a highball)

                    John

Not when I'm driving.

                    Harry
Wise.
             (To the others)
Drink? Oh, good, you've already helped yourselves.

                    Tom
Can't resist your bourbon, Harry.

                    Harry
             (Indicating a chair)
This suit you, John?

                    John
My favorite.
          (picks up newspaper)
How'd the Yankees make out?

                    Harry
Won again. Three to one.

                    Dick
Poor Red Sox.

                    John
Williams got the only run, I see, a homer. I can't understand how such a
good team loses so many games.

          (They ponder this for a moment)

                    Harry
          (Broaching a new subject)
I've been thinking over what you suggested last week, Tom. I'm disposed
to agree that it might be a good thing for all of us.

                    Dick
You mean this getting-things-out-of-our-system business?

                    Harry
Yes. You'll remember that Tom thought that it would be beneficial to us
all. Need to unload once in a while. Bad for us to keep anything bottled
up too long. I'm all for it. How about the rest of you?

                    Tom
Obviously I'm for it or I would never have mentioned it.

                    Dick
I'll tag along. How about you, John?

                    John
Well, I . . .

                    Harry
          (Quickly, overriding any objection)
Of course John's with us. Tom, as it was your suggestion, how about you
taking the lead?

                    Tom
Right. I've kept this quiet, as I guess you have the things you'll tell
us. I gamble. Oh, not just a tenth of a cent at bridge - I really gamble;
dice, roulette, cards - the works. Fortunately no one at the bank knows
it and fortunately gambling with other people's money doesn't interest me.
Also, I can afford it. But the strain of keeping it under my hat has been

                              Tom (con't)
terrific. Glad to share it.

                    (A pause while they ponder Tom's trouble)

Your turn, Dick.

                              Dick
                    (Blurting it out)
I drink! Of course you've seen me take a drink or two at a party or like
this. I don't mean that. About twice a year I go up to the cabin with a
case or two of whiskey and just soak it in. I don't shave or bathe - in
fact I'm just a sodden mass - a fine looking surgeon! After about a week
I've had enough and I get straightened out and that's that for another six
months. I hate it but there it is. Now you, too, know.

                    (Another pause)

                              Harry
You men have been frank and so shall I. It's women with me.

                    (Astonishment shows on their faces)

Yes, you can stare. Harry Hanson, pillar of the church, the perfect family
man with a lovely wife, fine children. I know what people think and say
about me and they might not believe this but it's true. I, too, periodically go off the track. I go to the Big City, hide away in a hotel and
have women. A series of them. After it's over, I return to my family, my
wife, whom I love dearly, and never think of another woman, not for many
months. And there you have it!

                    (Another pause)

Well, John, it's up to you.

                              John
                    (John has a strange look on his face -
                    he seems to be transported to another
                    world. He speaks with difficulty.)
No. I'm afraid . . . no, I better not.

                              Tom
Come, come. It'll do you good.

                              John
No. It's too terrible. You'll all hate me. You'll never speak to me
again.

                              Harry
You know we all agreed. Certainly you'll tell us. Why, see how much
better we all feel. Come on, now.

John

Well, if you really think . . .

Dick

It's the best thing.

John

If you'll promise . . .

(The others, simultaneously)

Tom	Dick	Harry
Certainly!	Of course!	Naturally, naturally!

John

It's like this. I'm a terrible gossip and I just can't wait to get home
to tell my wife everything.

(Consternation reigns among the others)

The Curtain Falls

ACT ONE, Scene 5

(The following morning. We are back in
John Smithers' office. When the curtain
rises Daisy is at her desk, busy sorting
the morning mail. After a moment or two
John enters.)

John
(Going to closet and hanging up his hat)
Good morning, Miss Caramel.

Daisy
(Making each dimple more attractive)
Good morning, Mr. Smithers!

John
Got the mail sorted?

(Daisy hands him the mail)

Good.
(He sits at his desk and opens his
letters. He reads one hurriedly and
passes it to Daisy.)
Just a short note answering this. The usual "sorry, conditions won't
permit further expansion at this time."
(Picks up another letter)
Well, well. Good thing we never finished that letter yesterday, Miss
Caramel. Here's one from ... ha, ha ... "supalia" ... ha, ha!

Daisy
Oh, how fortunate.

(The telephone rings - Daisy answers)

Daisy
John Smithers' office, Miss Caramel speaking.
(She listens)
He's right here, Miss Lammerton.
(She listens)
Certainly. Yes, I'll tell him.
(She hangs up)
(To John)
That was Miss Lammerton, Dr. Richard Bestor's office nurse. Dr. Bestor
won't be able to have lunch with you today. He left town suddenly and
won't be back for two weeks.

                         John
Oh?

                         Daisy
He went to his camp.

                         John
              (With a speculative gleam)
Ohhh?

              (Daisy returns to her desk)

              (John is lost in happy thought. His
               far-away look settles on Daisy and a
               new idea comes to him.)

                         John
Miss Caramel . . .

                         Daisy
Yes, Mr. Smithers?

                         John
Miss Caramel, has Mr. Harry Hanson ever

        etc.   etc.

Appendix B:
The Stage Manager's Working Prompt Script

JOHN X upstg, then
back, picks up phone ∧base,
X down, then to desk

                                   John
Whenever I find |that| the . . .   *PHONE*

                    (The telephone rings)

                                   Daisy
                    (Picking up the phone on her desk)
John Smithers' office. Miss Caramel speaking.   *S "L"*

                    (Hanson's angry voice is heard over the
                    phone, but the words are not distin-
                    guishable. Daisy holds the receiver
                    away from her ear, and each time Hanson
                    pauses for a breath Daisy tries to
                    speak.)

Yes, |Mr| Han . . .   *S "M"*

                    (Hanson has a fresh breath and goes
                    on talking for quite a while.)

But, if you'd |just| let me . . .   *S "N"*

                    (Again Hanson speaks)

                    (John has been quietly amused with
                    Daisy's predicament and decides to
                    offer his help. He takes the phone
                    from Daisy and shouts into it.)

                                   John   *← 1 BEAT*
                    (Shouting)
Listen, you old bag of wind, settle down! | | *S "O"*

                    (Hanson continues angrily but soon quiets
                    down, and the audience no longer can
                    hear him.)

                                   John (con't)
Fine! Fine! I'll see you tonight about eight-thirty. *WARN: PHONE*
                    (He hands the phone back to Daisy, who
                    replaces the receiver in its cradle.)   *CURTAIN*
Hanson can drown out a brass band when he gets started. Hard on the
ears . . .   *E 31, 32, 33*
                    (then, slyly)
          . . . especially such pretty pink ones, like yours. *SOUND P, Q*

                    (Daisy is embarrassed and, to tell   *: PORTAL (SW #1)*
                    the truth, a bit apprehensive.)   *: TURNTABLE (SW #2)*

                                   Daisy
Oh, Mister Smithers!   *(SITS)*

                    John
          (resuming office manner, Xes to his chair)
Yes, yes, ah . . . well, yes. I think we have time for one more letter.
          (HE sits)

                    Daisy
          (with no expression)
Certainly, Mr. Smithers.
          (takes notebook from drawer, picks up
           pencil, turns to John.)

                    John
          (dictating)
"Mr. A. Brush Wallaby"
          (aside to Daisy, small smile)
Put this on my personal stationery. You'll find his address in my
personal address book under Australia.
          (dictating)
"Dear Wally" comma "Long time no hear from" dash "what goes" question
mark. "Anxious to hear how things progress with all the supalia"
period. That's . . .
          (spelling)
. . . s - u - p - a - l - i - a . . .
          (explaining, self-consciously)
you know, plural diminutive of marsupial. Ha, ha! Well, ahem, ah . . .
          (resumes dictation)
"Molly and the kids pester the life out of me asking me when . . .   _PHONE_

          (TELELPHONE RINGS)

          (DAISY turns front, puts down notebook,
           answers phone.)

                    Daisy
          (into phone)
John Smithers' office, Miss Caramel speaking.   _SOUND P_
          (listens a moment)
Why, yes, Mr. Filibuster.

          (JOHN startled rises, Xes D.C., turns to
           Daisy, gestures wildly that he is "not in"
           has "gone out". DAISY pretends not to
           understand, continues to listen to phone.
           JOHN re-enacts "not in" business. SHE
           nods she understands. JOHN smiles, gets
           hat from closet, starts out, pats Daisy's
           shoulder, exits. DAISY alone, straightens   _CURTAIN_
           ~~HEAD~~   _E 31_
           STET   (SHE LOOKS UP)

WHEN CURT. IN	WORK LITE
" " "	PORTAL OUT (SW. #1)
" " "	S "P" (2)
WHEN PORTAL 6'	TURNTABLE TO "B" (SW #2)
T. TABLE TO "B"	PORTAL IN (SW. #1)
PORTAL IN	WORKS OUT
" "	E 32 (RAIN)
" "	FADE S "P"
ASM. CHECK ACTORS SOUND OUT	CURTAIN
CURTAIN ½ WAY	E 33
" " "	S "Q"

ACT ONE, Scene 4

(Shortly after eight the same evening.
Harry Hanson's workroom and hideaway.)

(AT RISE: HARRY sits in chair U.S. of
fireplace, reading newspaper.)

                              TOM (Offstage)
What a storm!

            (HARRY looks up.)

                              JEEVES (Off)
Very wet, sir. Yes, sir.

                         DICK (Off)
Better put those coats in the kitchen, Jeeves.

            (HARRY puts paper in chair, rises,
             crosses center.)

                              JEEVES (Off)
Yes, sir.

            (TOM ALBION and DICK BESTOR enter
             through door.)

WARN : ELEC 33A,34,35,36,37
       : SOUND R,S,T,U,V
       : PHONE

ACT ONE, Scene 4

(It is shortly after eight o'clock the
evening of the same day and we find our-
selves in Harry Hanson's house, in his
own workroom and hideaway, to be exact.
This is a small but comfortable room
with well-worn chairs and with shelves
for many books. A small table-desk is
at one side, a fireplace in the wall
opposite, a door leads to the rest of
the house. Through the darkened windows
we see vivid flashes of lightning, and
the thunder fairly shakes the house.
When the curtain rises we see Harry
sitting before the flickering fire reading the evening paper. Voices are
heard from offstage, and Harry putting
aside his paper, rises as Tom Albion
and Dick Bestor enter.)

                    Harry
Glad to see you could make it tonight, Tom.

          (They shake hands)

                    Tom
You know I never miss these sessions, Harry.

                    Harry
          (To Dick Bestor)
Richard Bestor, my old college roommate and lifelong pal. Richard
Bestor. How are you, Dick?

                    Dick
Fine, Harry, just fine.

          (They shake hands)

                    Harry
Make yourselves comfortable. John should be along any minute now. I
talked to him on the phone this afternoon - said he'd try to get here
by eight-thirty.

          (There is a bright flash of lightning,
           followed by a tremendous clap of
           thunder.)

Hope this storm doesn't keep him away.

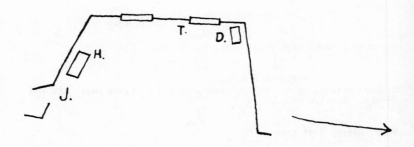

(JOHN'S ENTRANCE)

                              Dick
He hates driving in the rain.

                              Tom
I don't know that I blame him. That hill down from his house is really
treacherous during a storm.

                              Dick
We had a bad scare on it the other day when I was driving back from the
Canajoharie Country Club.

                              Harry
How did you get onto that road? We always use the Tallahassee-Spokane
Highway coming from the Club.

                              Dick
Bill Crunch's wife had their car and we were taking him home. It wouldn't
have been . . .   *PHONE*

                    (The telephone rings)
                              Harry
                    (answering)
Yes?
                    (He listens)
Oh, hello, Molly . . .

                    (Voices are heard offstage)

JOHN (OFF)
MISERABLE NIGHT, JEEVES
JEEVES
IT IS (THAT) SIR.

Just a second, Molly . . .
                    (He listens to the voices)
You don't have to worry, he just arrived.

                                                        E 34
                                                        S "S"

                    (John enters)
                    (W/ BOOK - WAVES TO OTHERS - BELOW DESK)
                              Harry (con't)
                    (into phone)
One minute and I'll put him on.
                    (Hands phone to John)
It's Molly, John.

   (X.L OF DESK)   John
                    (into phone)   *(T. JOIN D. AT BAR - BOTH GET DRINKS) TOOK IT*
Hello, dear.   *NO, NO TROUBLE AT ALL.*
                    (He listens)   *VERY CAREFULLY*
~~Now just relax and take it easy - I'll be OK.~~   *(T.C.)*
                    (Listens. Harry signals him that he   *NOW JUST RELAX AND*
                    would like to say something to Molly.) *TAKE IT EASY - I'LL*
Certainly, dear, certainly. Harry wants to talk to you again. *BE OK.*
                    (Passes phone to Harry)
                    (X TO FIRE)

Harry adds seltzer to glass — pre-set by Dick

Harry
(into phone)
Molly, now don't you worry. This storm will be over in a half hour . . .

(Terrific lightning and thunder)

E 35
S "T"

. . . at least I think it will be. Everything's under control. Yes . . .
yes . . . 'Right! Goodbye.
(He hangs up)—(T.C)

John
Molly gets into quite a state on nights like this if I'm out in it.
Spends most of her time on the phone calling the neighbors.
(H.X TO RADIO - JR)
Tom (XC)
Don't blame her. Dick was just telling us he had a bad time on that hill
of yours the other day.
(H. AT RADIO)
Dick
Fortunately we were just creeping along. Even so we turned completely
around. Nothing else in sight and stayed on the road. Lucky. Glad I'm
~~within~~ walking ~~distance~~ tonight, ~~You too, eh, Tom?~~ AREN'T YOU, TOM?

Tom

You bet!

E 36
S "U"

John
Yes, Molly worries and hangs onto the phone – does all day, anyway, storm
or no storm.

Harry
(Who has been trying the radio,
abandons it) – XLC)
Nothing but static. Drink, John?
(He starts to mix a highball)

John
Not when I'm driving.

Harry
Wise.
(To the others)
Drink? Oh, good, you've already helped yourselves.

Tom
Can't resist your bourbon, Harry.

E 37
S "V"

Harry
(Indicating a chair)
This suit you, John?

Harry puts down drink on desk, Xes & shuts door, returns to desk, gets drink.

Alternate line for Dick "You mean this getting-things-out-of-our-systems business?"

T.

J.

H.

D. D

John

My favorite.
> (picks up newspaper)

How'd the Yankees make out? *(SITS - READS)*

GRABBED ANOTHER

Harry

~~Won again.~~ Three to one. *(X TO DESK)*

(SIT DL)

Dick

Poor Red Sox.

John

Williams got the only run, I see, a homer. I can't understand how such a
good team loses so many games.

> (They ponder this for a moment)   *WARN: ELEC. 38*
>   *: SOUND W*

Harry
> (Broaching a new subject)

I've been thinking over what you suggested last week, Tom. I'm disposed
to agree that it might be a good thing for all of us.

←⎯⎯⎯→ CONFESSION

Dick

You mean this ~~getting-things-out-of-our-system~~ business?

Harry

Yes. You'll remember that Tom thought that it would be beneficial to us
all. Need to unload once in a while. Bad for us to keep anything bottled
up too long. I'm all for it. How about the rest of you?
(SIT)

Tom

Obviously I'm for it or I would never have mentioned it.

Dick

I'll **tag** along. How about you, John?

John

Well, I . . .

Harry
> (Quickly, overriding any objection)

Of course John's with us. Tom, as it was your suggestion, how about you
taking the lead?

Tom

Right. I've kept this quiet, as I guess you have the things you'll tell
us. I gamble. Oh, not just a tenth of a cent at bridge - I really gamble;
dice, roulette, cards - the works. Fortunately no one at the bank knows
it and fortunately gambling with other people's money doesn't interest me.
Also, I can afford it. But the strain of keeping it under my hat has been

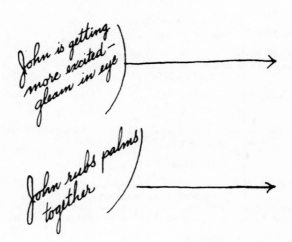

John is getting
more excited —
gleam in eye

John rubs palms
together

Tom (con't)
terrific. Glad to share it. *(X TO BAR POUR DRINK)*

(A pause while they ponder Tom's trouble) *AS DRINK FULL E 38*

S "W"

Your turn, Dick.

(T. SIT L.C.)

Dick
(Blurting it out)
I drink! Of course you've seen me take a drink or two at a party or like
this. I don't mean that. About twice a year I go up to the cabin with a
case or two of whiskey and just soak it in. I don't shave or bathe - in
fact I'm just a sodden mass - a fine looking surgeon! After about a week
I've had enough and I get straightened out and that's that for another six
months. I hate it but there it is. Now you, too, know.

(RISE - PUT DRINK MANTLE - SIT)
(Another pause)

Harry *(TAKE GLASS TO DESK)*
You men have been frank and so shall I. It's women with me. *←(SIT)*
(Astonishment shows on their faces)

Yes, you can stare. Harry Hanson, pillar of the church, the perfect family
man with a lovely wife, fine children. I know what people think and say
about me and they might not believe this but it's true. I, too, periodically go off the track. I go to the Big City, hide away in a hotel and
have women. A series of them. After it's over, I return to my family, my
wife, whom I love dearly, and never think of another woman, not for many
months. And there you have it!

WARN : CURTAIN
: ELEC. 39, 40
(Another pause)
: SOUND X, Y

Well, John, it's up to you.
: PORTAL (SW#1)
: TURNTABLE (SW#2)
: PHONE

John
(John has a strange look on his face -
he seems to be transported to another
world. He speaks with difficulty.)
No. I'm afraid . . . no, I better not.

Tom
Come, come. It'll do you good.

John
No. It's too terrible. You'll all hate me. You'll never speak to me
again.

Harry
You know we all agreed. Certainly you'll tell us. Why, see how much
better we all feel. Come on, now.

orght margin:

John

Well, if you really think . . .

Dick

It's the best thing.

John

If you'll promise . . .

(The others, simultaneously)

Tom	Dick	Harry
Certainly!	Of course!	Naturally, naturally!

John

It's like this. ~~I'm a terrible gossip and I just can't wait to get home to tell my wife everything.~~ *I JUST CAN'T WAIT 'TIL MORNING.*
I'M A GOSSIP (1 BEAT) _____ *(FAST) CURTAIN*

(Consternation reigns among the others)

E 39

S "X"

The Curtain Falls

CURTAIN DOWN	*WORK LITE*
	S "Y"
	PORTAL OUT (SW#1)
PORTAL 6' OFF.	*T. TABLE TO "A" (SW#2)*
T. TABLE TO "A"	*PORTAL IN (SW#1)*
	A.S.M. CHECK ACTORS FLASH Q's
	WORK LITE OUT
	FADE S "Y"
SOUND OUT	*CURTAIN UP*
C. HEAD HI.	*E 40*

ACT ONE, Scene 5

(The following morning. We are back in
John Smithers' office. When the curtain
rises Daisy is at her desk, busy sorting
the morning mail. After a moment or two
John enters.)

John
(Going to closet and hanging up his hat)
Good morning, Miss Caramel.

Daisy
(Making each dimple more attractive)
Good morning, Mr. Smithers!

John

Got the mail sorted?

(Daisy hands him the mail)

Good.
(He sits at his desk and opens his
letters. He reads one hurriedly and
passes it to Daisy.)
Just a short note answering this. The usual "sorry, conditions won't
permit further expansion at this time."
(Picks up another letter)
Well, well. Good thing we never finished that letter yesterday, Miss
Caramel. Here's one from ... ha, ha ... "supalia" ... ha, ha!

Daisy
Oh, how fortunate.   PHONE

(The telephone rings - Daisy answers)
(D.X TO DESK- NOTEBOOK ON DESK)
Daisy
John Smithers' office, Miss Caramel speaking.
(She listens)
He's right here, Miss Lammerton.
(She listens) - (J. PANTO. "NO")
Certainly. Yes, I'll tell him.
(She hangs up)
(To John)
That was Miss Lammerton, Dr. Richard Bestor's office nurse. Dr. Bestor
won't be able to have lunch with you today. He left town suddenly and
won't be back for two weeks.

                    John
Oh?

                    Daisy
He went to his camp.

                    John
          (With a speculative gleam)
Ohhh?

          (Daisy returns to her desk)

          (John is lost in happy thought. His
          far-away look settles on Daisy and a
          new idea comes to him.)

                    John
Miss Caramel . . .

                    Daisy
Yes, Mr. Smithers?

                    John
Miss Caramel, has Mr. Harry Hanson ever

          etc.   etc.

Decanter, 4 glasses, soda siphon

Phone

Newspaper

Door OPEN

Shades UP

Fireplace FLICKER

Rain

ACT ONE, Scene 5

Letters on Daisy's desk

etc.

etc.

PROPERTIES

ACT ONE, Scene 4

ON STAGE

       Table-desk, stg R.
           Blotter, inkstand, phone, calendar
       Straight chair by desk
       Console radio, magazine on top
       Green brocade drapes on windows
       Roller shades on windows
       Book cases and books (not practical)
       Cellarette
           Whiskey, 4 glasses, ice, siphon (all practical)
       2 comfortable armchairs
       1 armchair - smaller
       Evening Newspaper

OFFSTAGE & HAND

       Book off D.R. (JOHN)

ACT ONE, Scene 5

       etc.   etc.

Appendix C:
The Finished Prompt Script

John

Whenever I find that the . . .

(TELEPHONE RINGS)

Daisy
(picks up phone from her desk)
John Smithers' office, Miss Caramel speaking.

(HANSON'S voice is heard over the phone.
No words are discernible, but the tone
of his voice is angry and excited.
DAISY holds receiver away from ear when
he speaks and each time HANSON pauses
DAISY tries to speak.)

Yes, Mr. Han . . .

(HANSON again)

But, if you'd just let me . . .

(HANSON again)

(JOHN , quietly amused, picks up his
extension from his desk and takes charge.)

John
Listen, you old bag of wind, settle down!

(DAISY replaces her phone - starts
writing in her notebook.)

(HANSON continues angrily - after a
moment, quiets down.)

(JOHN rises, walks upstage to limit of
phone receiver wire, comes back, picks
up phone base, walks dnstage to limit
of wire, Xes back to his desk, listens.)

John (con't)
Fine! Fine! I'll see you tonight about eight-thirty.
(HE replaces phone, Xes to L. of Daisy.)
Hanson can drown out a brass band when he gets started. Hard on the
ears . . .
(slyly)
especially such pretty pink ones, like yours.

Daisy
(embarrassed, looks at desk)
Oh, Mister Smithers!

                              John
                    (resuming office manner, Xes to his chair)
Yes, yes, ah . . . well, yes. I think we have time for one more letter.
                    (HE sits)

                              Daisy
                    (with no expression)
Certainly, Mr. Smithers.
                    (takes notebook from drawer, picks up
                     pencil, turns to John.)

                              John
                    (dictating)
"Mr. A. Brush Wallaby"
                    (aside to Daisy, small smile)
Put this on my personal stationery. You'll find his address in my
personal address book under Australia.
                    (dictating)
"Dear Wally" comma "Long time no hear from" dash "what goes" question
mark. "Anxious to hear how things progress with all the supalia"
period. That's . . .
                    (spelling)
. . . s - u - p - a - l - i - a . . .
                    (explaining, self-consciously)
you know, plural diminutive of marsupial. Ha, ha! Well, ahem, ah . . .
                    (resumes dictation)
"Molly and the kids pester the life out of me asking me when . . .

                    (TELELPHONE RINGS)

                    (DAISY turns front, puts down notebook,
                     answers phone.)

                              Daisy
                    (into phone)
John Smithers' office, Miss Caramel speaking.
                    (listens a moment)
Why, yes, Mr. Filibuster.

                    (JOHN startled rises, Xes D.C., turns to
                     Daisy, gestures wildly that he is "not in"
                     has "gone out". DAISY pretends not to
                     understand, continues to listen to phone.
                     JOHN re-enacts "not in" business. SHE
                     nods she understands. JOHN smiles, gets
                     hat from closet, starts out, pats Daisy's
                     shoulder, exits. DAISY alone, straightens

things on her desk, as she continues
to listen to Filibuster.)

CURTAIN - MEDIUM SLOW

(During the scene change there are no house
lights but over the loud speakers in the
auditorium Filibuster's voice may be heard.
Most of what he says is a confused jumble of
words with occasional clear passages. Daisy's
voice comes through weakly at intervals,"Yes,
Mr. Filibuster" and "No, Mr. Filibuster"
being the extent of what she says. The sound
dies away just as the curtain rises on Scene 4.)

ACT ONE, Scene 4

(The curtain has just left the floor when
there is a terrific clap of thunder.
After it rises Harry Hanson's workroom
is revealed. It is shortly after eight,
the same evening. It is raining.)

(The room is small and comfortable with
well-worn chairs, and shelves for many
books. D.R. an open door to hall. In
U.R. corner a console radio. Above door
against R. wall a table-desk with straight
chair. Built-in bookcase in R. wall. Two
windows upstage with bookcase between.
Curtains not drawn. In U.L. corner a
cellarette with glasses, decanter, soda,
ice ready. Fireplace with fire burning
in C. of L. wall. Above fireplace facing
D.S., easy chair. D.L. against wall
facing Stg R., easy chair. C. windsor
chair facing fireplace.)

(AT RISE: HARRY, in gray slacks and smoking
jacket, sits in chair U.S. of fireplace,
reading newspaper.)

                    Tom (offstage)
What a storm!

                 (HARRY looks up)
                 (LIGHTNING & THUNDER)

                    Jeeves (off)
Very wet, sir. Yes, sir.

                    Dick (off)
Better put those coats in the kitchen, Jeeves.

                 (HARRY puts paper in chair, rises, Xes C.)

                    Jeeves (off)
Yes, sir.

                 (TOM ALBION and DICK BESTOR enter thru door)

                 (Tom Albion is a man of 35, tall and dark.
                 He wears a tweed suit. Dick Bestor, about 45,
                 is short and stocky with iron-gray hair,
                 wears a dark blue business suit.)

                    Harry
Glad you could make it tonight, Tom.

          (THEY shake hands)

                    Tom
You know .I never miss these sessions, Harry.
          (Xes U.L.)

                    Harry
          (with mock formality)
Richard Bestor! Doctor Richard Bestor!
          (then, easily)
How are you, Dick, you old sawbones?

                    Dick
Fine, Harry, just fine!

          (THEY shake hands. DICK Xes to fireplace)

                    Harry
          (still C.)
Make yourselves comfortable. John should be along any minute now. I
talked to him on the phone this afternoon - said he'd try to get here by
eight-thirty.

          (LIGHTNING & THUNDER)

Hope this storm doesn't keep him away.
          (Xes up to R. window)

                    Dick
          (warming hands, back to room)
He hates driving in the rain.

                    Tom
          (X to L. window)
I don't know that I blame him. That hill down from his house is really
treacherous during a storm.

                    Dick
          (turns to others)
We had a bad scare on it the other day when I was driving back from the
Canajoharie Country Club.

                    Harry
          (Xing to L. of chair L.C.)
How did you get onto that road? We always use the Tallahassee-Spokane
Highway coming from the Club.

                    Dick
              (Xing to cellarette)
Bill Crunch's wife had their car and we were taking him home. It
wouldn't have been . . .

              (TELEPHONE RINGS)

                    Harry
              (Xes to desk R., answers)
Yes?
              (listens)
Oh, hello, Molly . . .

                    John (offstage)
Miserable night, Jeeves.

              (LIGHTNING & THUNDER)

                    Jeeves (off)
It is that, sir.

                    Harry
              (hearing voices off)
Just a second, Molly . . .

                    John (off)
Hope it stops soon.

                    Harry
              (into phone)
You don't have to worry, he just arrived.

              (JOHN enters wearing same suit as in
              Scene 3. He carries a book. HE
              waves "hello" to others. Xes to
              below desk.)

One minute, Molly, and I'll put him on.
              (hands phone to John)
It's Molly, John.
              (HARRY Xes to C.)

                    John
              (Xes to L. of desk, puts down book)
              (Into phone)
Hello, dear.
              (listens)

              (TOM joins DICK at cellarette - both
               get drinks)

John (con't)
No, no trouble at all. Took it very carefully.
(listens - turns C.)
Now just relax and take it easy - I'll be OK.
(listens. HARRY signals he wants to
talk to her again.)
Certainly, dear, certainly. Harry wants to talk to you again.
(gives HARRY phone - Xes to fireplace)

Harry
(into phone)
Molly, now don't you worry. This storm will be over in a halfhour . . .

(LIGHTNING & THUNDER)

at least I think it will be. Everything's under control. Yes . . .
yes . . . Right! Goodbye.
(hangs up - turns C.)

John.
(back to fire)
Molly gets into quite a state on nights like this if I'm out in it.
Spends most of her time on the phone calling the neighbors.

(HARRY Xes to radio U.R.)

Tom
(Xing U.C. with highball)
Don't blame her. Dick was just telling us he had a bad time on that hill
of yours the other day.

(HARRY fiddles with radio)

Dick
(X to John - has highball)
Fortunately we were just creeping along. Even so we turned completely
around. Nothing else in sight, and we stayed on the road. Lucky. Glad
I'm walking tonight, aren't you, Tom?

(LIGHTNING & THUNDER)

Tom
You bet!

John
Yes, Molly worries and hangs onto the phone - does it all day, anyway,
storm or no storm. Ha, ha!

                    Harry
          (Has been at radio U.R. corner, now
           Xes to U.L.)
Nothing but static. Drink, John?
          (starts to mix highball)

                    John
Not when I'm driving.

                    Harry
Wise.
          (to others)
Drink? Oh, good, you've already helped yourselves.

                    Tom
          (X & sit chair L.C.)
Can't resist your bourbon, Harry.

          (LIGHTNING & THUNDER)

                    Harry
          (indicating chair U.S. fireplace)
This suit you, John?

                    John
          (Xing to chair)
My favorite.
          (picks up newspaper)
How'd the Yankees make out?
          (sits - reads)

                    Harry
          (Xes to desk - puts down drink)
Grabbed another. Three to one.

                    Dick
          (sits chair D.L.)
Poor Red Sox.

          (HARRY Xes to door, closes it. Xes
           back to desk, picks up drink.)

                    John
          (with newspaper)
Williams got their only run, I see; a homer. I can't understand how
such a good team loses so many games.

          (Pause - each with own thoughts)

                    Harry
          (Pulls desk chair to D.C.)
I've been thinking over what you suggested last week, Tom. I'm disposed
to agree that it might be a good thing for all of us.

                              Dick
You mean this getting-things-out-of-our-system business?

                              Harry
Yes. You'll remember that Tom thought that it would be beneficial to us
all. Need to unload once in a while. Bad for us to keep anything bottled
up too long. I'm all for it.
                    (sits)
How about the rest of you?

                              Tom
Obviously I'm for it or I would never have suggested it.

                              Dick
I'll tag along. How about you, John?

                              John
Well, I . . .

                              Harry
                    (quickly - overriding)
Of course John's with us. Tom, as it was your suggestion, how about
you taking the lead?

                    (THEY have formed a group-of-three downstage
                    of John and only occasionally throw him a
                    glance. JOHN, unnoticed, grows more and
                    more excited as the others tell their stories.
                    When each finishes and there is general move-
                    ment and looking around, JOHN freezes.)

                              Tom
Right. I've kept this quiet, as I guess you have the things you'll tell
us. I gamble. Oh, not just a tenth-of-a-cent-at-bridge sort of thing -
I really gamble; dice, roulette, cards - the works. Fortunately no one
at the bank knows it and fortunately gambling with other people's money
doesn't interest me. Also, I can afford it. But the strain of keeping
it under my hat has been terrific. Glad to share it.

                    (LIGHTNING & THUNDER)

                    (TOM Xes to cellarette, gets more whiskey)

                    (A pause - JOHN is very quiet)

                              Tom (con't)
Your turn, Dick.
                    (Xes and sits L.C.)

                              Dick
                    (Blurting it out)
I drink! Of course you've seen me take a drink or two at a party or like

Dick (con't)

this. I don't mean that. About twice a year I go up to the cabin with a case or two of whiskey and just soak it in. I don't shave or bathe - in fact I'm just a sodden mass - a fine looking surgeon! After about a week I've had enough and I get straightened out and that's that for another six months. I hate it but there it is. Now you, too, know.
(HE rises, puts glass on mantel, sits again.)

(A pause - JOHN has gleam in eye)

Harry
(who has gone to desk, leaves glass, returns)
You men have been frank and so shall I.
(sits)
It's women with me.

(Astonishment from ALL -
JOHN rubs palms together)

Yes, you can stare. Harry Hanson, pillar of the church, the perfect family man with a lovely wife, fine children. I know what people think and say about me and they might not believe this but it's true. I, too, periodically go off the track. I go to the Big City, hide away in a hotel and have women. A series of them. After it's over I return to my family, whom I love dearly, and never think of another woman, except my wife, for many months. And there you have it!

(Another pause)

Well, John, it's up to you.

(ALL turn to John)

John
(with difficulty)
No. I'm afraid . . . no, I better not.

Tom
Come, come. It'll do you good.

John
No. It's too terrible. You'd all hate me. You'd never speak to me again.

Harry
You know we all agreed. Certainly you'll tell us. Why, see how much better we all feel. Come on, now.

                              John
Well, if you really think . . .

                              Dick
It's the best thing.

                              John
If you'll promise . . .

               (ALL - simultaneously)

      Tom   Dick   Harry
   Certainly!   Of course!   Naturally! Naturally!

                              John
It's like this. I just can't wait 'til morning. I'm a gossip!

               (Consternation)

               (LIGHTNING & THUNDER, FORTISSIMO)

                    FAST   CURTAIN

               (Between the scenes there are no house lights.
               The sound of thunder rolls about the auditorium
               coming from the loud speakers. The thunder soon
               blends into the roar of city traffic. The traffic
               noises become more and more staccato and are dis-
               placed by the clackety-clack of a typewriter. The
               typing noise fades away as the curtain rises on
               Scene 5.)

ACT ONE, Scene 5

(John Smithers' office, the following
morning. It is as we last saw it except
that it looks "cleaned" and "arranged".
Letters that were scattered are now in
neat piles, chairs are squared up along
side of the desks, the window shades are
even, wastebaskets are empty, etc.

(AT RISE: DAISY is sitting at her desk,
sorting mail. SHE has just finished
when JOHN enters from R.)

                    John
          (Xing to closet, hangs up hat)
Good morning, Miss Caramel.

                    Daisy
          (smiling)
Good morning, Mr. Smithers..

          etc.   etc.

PROPERTY PLOT

Act One, Scene 4

Stage Right Wall (D.S.R. to Up)
Over door, mounted fish (small)
Desk C. of wall
    On top of desk:
        Desk set
        Phone
        Student lamp (practical, see LIGHTS)
Over desk, on wall
    Framed antique map, no glass
Up stage of desk - built-in book shelves
    Books - not practical
In U.R. corner - Console radio (not practical)
    6 magazines on top

Back wall (R. to L.)
R.C. of wall - window
    Heavy green velour drapes with valance
    Dark green roller shade - halfway down
C. of wall - built-in book shelves
    Books - not practical
L.C. of wall - window
    Ditto other window

Stage Left Wall (Up stage L. to Down)
In U.L. corner - Cellarette
    On top, ready to use - all practical
        Silver tray holding: glass ice bucket with cube
            ice, silver ice tongs, decanter of whiskey,
            stopper, 4 highball glasses, siphon of
            soda (Sparklet)
        Small lamp (practical - see LIGHTS)
On wall above cellarette - small hunting print
C. of wall - fireplace
    On mantel - 2 small loving cups, small model sailing
        ship
On wall above fireplace - mounted sailfish
Down stg fireplace, against wall - large green overstuffed chair
On wall over chair - hunting print
Down stg of chair - floor lamp - practical (see LIGHTS)

Up stage of fireplace, facing front, large brown overstuffed chair
    Newspaper in seat
L.C. facing fireplace - mahogany windsor chair
L. of desk - mahogany straight chair

Carpet - wall to wall neutral green

Offstage D.R.
    Book, **The Houses In Between** (JOHN)

LIGHT PLOT

Note to reader: At the beginning of the light plot there is a list of all equipment, including each instrument and its number, where it is placed, its color gelatine, its focus, and the area it lights. And so for each scene it is not necessary to repeat this information—only the instrument number, intensity, and change need be noted.

LIGHT PLOT
ACT ONE, Scene 4

FRONT LIGHTS:
    #3, 4, 5, 6, 7, 8, 9, 10, all 3/4 up

1st PIPE: #4 -- Full
           5 -- Full
           6 -- 1/2 up
           7 -- Full
         10 -- 3/4 up
         11 -- Full
         13 -- 1/2 up
         14 -- Full
         15 -- Full
    X-rays -- Amber only - 1/4 up

OVER DOOR R. (off):
    4-compartment strip, 25 watt, frosted light amber

DESK STAGE R.:
    Student lamp - practical

CELLARETTE U.L. CORNER:
    Small lamp, parchment shade - practical

DOWN STAGE L.:
    Floor lamp, parchment shade - practical

RAIN EFFECT:
    Outside windows Up stge - thruout scene

FIREPLACE FLICKER:
    Thruout scene

LIGHTNING FLASH
    Outside windows - thruout scene on cue

NO FOOTS

NO CHANGE OF LIGHT ON STAGE

Scenery Plot

NOTE TO READER: This will be a brief, informative description of how the scenery is handled. In this case mention of the revolving stage (turntable), of which backings are flown or run, of any specialties such as quick-change rooms, together with small-scale drawings of the ground plans and full stage photos of the settings, should suffice.

Many designers are loathe to permit any use of their work other than the original production without further remuneration. The general manager should be consulted as to what information, diagrams, etc., the designer will permit in the Finished Prompt Script as this script may be the basis of stock productions, amateur productions and the like.

ACT ONE, Sc. 4

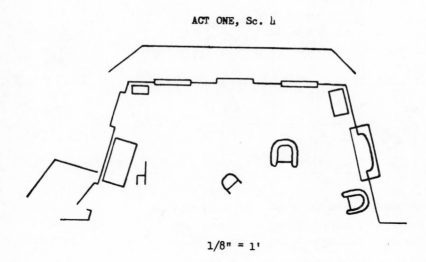

1/8" = 1'

181

ACT ONE, Scene 3, (Con't)

#	COUNTS	CUE	DESCRIPTION	MARK
31	3	with CURTAIN	FRONTS OUT	OUT

Scene 4

#	COUNTS	CUE	DESCRIPTION	MARK
32		PRESENT before CURT. up	Rain Effect	FULL
33	3	Head High	FRONTS UP	7
33A	Bump	"by eight-thirty"	Lightning Special	FULL
34	"	"It is that, sir."	" "	"
35	"	"in a half-hour"	" "	"
36	"	"you bet"	" "	"
37	"	"Your bourbon, Harry"	" "	"
38	"	Bus: As drink full	" "	"
39	Bump	with CURTAIN	Lightning Spcl. with fronts follow out	FULL flw. to OUT

Scene 5

#	COUNTS	CUE	DESCRIPTION	MARK
40	3	Head High	FRONTS UP	FULL
etc.	etc.	etc.	etc.	etc.

NOTE TO READER: To this list of cues should be appended a list
of the equipment, including placement of instruments, gels, etc.

As with the Scenery plot, however, the General Manager
should be consulted as to what information the designer will
permit to be used.

182

SOUND CUES

ACT ONE, Scene 3 (Con't)

#	CUE	DECK	DESCRIPTION	SPEAKER	VOL.
L	"Miss Caramel speaking"	1	Hanson's voice	In Desk	8
M	"Yes, Mr. Han..."	2	" "	" "	8
N	"you'd just let me..."	1	" "	" "	8
O	"...settle down"(Beat)	2	" "	" "	12 Fade to out - 6 counts

Scene 4

P	On Curtain Down	1	Filibuster's voice	Fronts	10-Fade out on cue-4 cts.
Q	Head high	2	Thunder	Upstage	14
R	"by eight-thirty"	2	"	"	14
S	"It is that, sir"	2	"	"	14
T	"in a half-hour"	2	"	"	14
U	"You bet."	2	"	"	14
V	"Your bourbon, Harry"	2	"	"	14
W	Bus: As drink full	2	"	"	16
X	With Curtain	2	"	"	18

Scene 5

Y	Curtain Down	1	Typing-Office noise	Fronts	10-Fade on cue - 4 cts.

NOTE TO READER: As with the Light Plot, a list of equipment, including speaker placement will be appended.

183

COSTUME PLOT

COSTUME PLOT

Act One, Scene 4

HARRY:

    Maroon, solid-colored smoking jacket
    Dark gray flannel slacks
    White negligee shirt - no tie
    Plain brown socks
    Dark brown loafers

TOM:

    Brown tweed suit
    White shirt, button down collar - bow tie
    Argyle socks
    Dark brown oxfords

DICK:

    Dark blue worsted suit
    Light blue shirt - white line
    Black and crimson striped four-in-hand
    Dark socks
    Black oxfords

JOHN:

(Same as Act One, Scene 3)

Appendix D:
Selected Union Rules

Any attempt to list all the rules of the various theatrical unions would certainly be doomed to failure. First, the mere volume of such a listing would extend this handbook beyond practical length. Also, union rules undergo constant revision and change. Only the spirit of the rules is meant to be conveyed here. Remember, the Equity rule book and the IATSE rule book should be read thoroughly and referred to constantly. If there is a question, the Equity Representative or the IA Business Agent is always available for the price of a phone call.

ACTORS' EQUITY RULES AND TRADITIONS

Contracts:

1. The stage manager does not work, even before rehearsals, without a contract stipulating his salary. Consequently, a stage manager always works for full pay.
2. Stage managers do not act parts.
3. Stage managers are not regular understudies, but may substitute in extreme emergencies.
4. Assistant stage managers must have contracts, and work for full salary at all times.
5. Assistant stage managers may act parts and/or understudy. (In musical productions the first assistant may not.)
6. Actors may not rehearse without a contract.

Rehearsals:

1. Notify Equity of the date, time and place of the first rehearsal.
2. Prepare a list of all actors, understudies and stage managers. This list should be sent to the Equity representative several days before the first rehearsal.
3. Receive from the Equity representative the Deputy Election Sheet(s) and medical and life insurance forms.
4. The rehearsal pay for all actors is the basic minimum salary (which is determined each season on a scale previously agreed to by the League and Equity). Stage managers receive full salary from the first day they report for work.
5. The rehearsal week (except for the last week before the first performance) is six days out of seven.

187

6. First day of rehearsal is the day on which any actor is first called to attend a rehearsal. A reading of the play, as a preliminary to walking rehearsals, is considered a rehearsal. All actors are not necessarily called the same day. Thus the first rehearsal day for each actor need not be the same. Either a reading by the actors or a reading to the actors (by the director or anyone else) is considered a reading of the play.

   (There is another form of "reading the play." This is a formal reading to enable the producer to evaluate a manuscript. Actors are hired at a nominal, but Equity-established and controlled salary, for this one reading and one purpose. This is not the type of reading referred to when "reading the play" is used in conjunction with regular rehearsals of the play.)

7. An actor who is called for a rehearsal, and who appears at rehearsal, even though he may not rehearse, or may be dismissed immediately, is considered to have rehearsed that day.

8. Equity rules provide for a five-day probationary period. (Three days for chorus.) If an actor is engaged within seven days of the first rehearsal, the producer may discharge him before the end of the fifth (or third) day with no obligation except to pay him for the time he has been a member of the rehearsing company plus any money legally due him. The actor must be given his notice personally and in writing before the end of the fifth (third) rehearsal day.

9. Actors under a "Principal" or "white" contract may rehearse four weeks (five weeks, if the production is a musical) at rehearsal salary. Actors under a "Chorus" or "pink" contract may rehearse six weeks at rehearsal salary.

   The producer may opt to extend the rehearsal period by ten days by paying one-sixth of the rehearsal salary for each of the first three days and the last seven days at minimum salary. (Road or New York, whichever applies.)

   After the rehearsal days have been used or after the first paid public performance (whichever is soonest) the actor will be paid his full contractual salary.

188

Except: If an out-of-town tryout tour is made, any unused rehearsal days may be used between the time the company returns to New York and the first performance in New York. One rehearsal day may also be used in each new city on the tryout tour (providing that there are unused days).

10. Rehearsal Hours.

   a. The only rule pertaining to the stage manager is that he have an eight-hour rest period between days. Otherwise he is on call at all times.

   b. The rehearsal week is six days out of seven. One day off must be given each calendar week. The day off may be changed from week to week (Monday the first week, Thursday the second week); however, it is simple courtesy to let the actors know which days have been decided upon as far in advance as possible, so that they may make doctors' appointments and the like.

   c. Until the last week of rehearsal actors' rehearsals are limited to eight-and-one-half consecutive hours. Of these eight-and-one-half hours, one-and-one-half hours must be allotted as a meal (or rest) period.

   d. Under no circumstances may a rehearsal session exceed five hours without a meal (or rest) break.

   e. Chorus members and principals working with chorus are entitled to a five-minute rest period each hour.

   Sample legal rehearsal schedule for all actors during the first three (or four) weeks:

   > 10 A.M. to 12 Noon — Rehearsal
   > 12 Noon to 1:30 P.M. — Meal Period
   > 1:30 P.M. to 6 P.M. — Rehearsal

   The above is seven out of eight-and-one-half consecutive hours. And some illegal schedules:

   > 10 A.M. to 1 P.M. — Rehearsal
   > 1 P.M. to 4 P.M. — Meal Period
   > 4 P.M. to 8 P.M. — Rehearsal

189

or

10 A.M. to 11:30 A.M. — Rehearsal
11:30 A.M. to 1 P.M. — Meal Period
1 P.M. to 6:30 P.M. — Rehearsal

In the first example the eight-and-one-half consecutive hour rule has been broken (although the actors have actually only rehearsed for seven hours) and in the second example the five hour limit has been exceeded.

It is possible to stagger rehearsal hours so that no individual actor rehearses over the allotted time. For example:

10 A.M. to 12 Noon — Rehearsal: Group A
12 Noon to 1:30 P.M. — Meal Period
1:30 P.M. to 6:30 P.M. — Rehearsal: Groups A & B
6:30 P.M. — Dismiss Group A
6:30 P.M. to 8 P.M. — Meal Period: Group B
8 P.M. to 10 P.M. — Rehearsal: Groups B & C
10 P.M. — Dismiss Group B
10 P.M. to 11:30 A.M. — Meal Period: Group C
11:30 P.M. to 4:30 A.M. — Rehearsal: Group C

The stage managers would have to work all three shifts, although, if the rehearsal continued until 4:30 in the morning, the stage managers would not be required to report to rehearsal the next day until 1:30 in the afternoon. If this type of schedule is contemplated (and the above example is an extreme), the stage manager should schedule his staff so that each rehearsal is adequately stage managed, but also that each stage manager receives enough rest to operate efficiently.

f. Principals are permitted two two-hour costume fitting calls during the rehearsal period. However, they must be continuous with rehearsal time and not scheduled on the day off. For example, if an actor is scheduled to rehearse at noon, he may be called to the costume shop at 10 A.M. for a fitting. On such a day he would be dismissed at 8:30 P.M. Chorus members are permitted three such two-hour calls. Any further costume fitting must be scheduled during rehearsal hours, or paid for at overtime.

g. The final week before the first public performance is made up of "10 out of 12" hour days. That is, a twelve-hour span containing ten rehearsal hours. The five-hour session rule remains as does the minimum of one-and-a-half hours for meal break. And, of course, proper rest breaks (five minutes per hour for chorus). The rest period between the end of work one day and the beginning of work the following day must be twelve hours.—*Except* for the twenty-four hours preceding the first public performance, when the rest period must be at least nine hours.

h. After the out-of-town tryout opening the work day is ten out of twelve consecutive hours (allow three hours for performance) and operates on a seven-day-a-week schedule. At some point in the first three weeks out of town a full day off must be given. Also, one day off in the second three weeks. After the first six weeks out of town (a long tryout) one day off for the company in each two weeks must be given.

i. If the play opens in New York without an out-of-town tryout, rehearsals may be held for the first two weeks after the preview opening utilizing ten out of twelve consecutive hours (including performance). No Sunday rehearsals are permitted in New York after the preview opening. After two weeks the work day reverts to seven out of eight-and-one-half consecutive hours, including performance, until the official New York opening.

j. Remember, if in doubt, consult the Equity rule book, the Equity Deputy and/or the Equity Representative.

Rehearsals After The New York Opening.

Principal actors and understudies are limited to twelve hours of rehearsal per week after the New York opening. Chorus rehearsals are limited to eight hours per week on material already in the show. If new material is put in the show or an emergency cast replacement should occur, chorus members may rehearse twelve hours. If an actor has a firm commitment of employment, he is not required to attend rehearsal on a day he is otherwise employed.

Equity Deputy

It is customary to elect the Equity deputy on the fifth (or third) day of rehearsal, although there is no rule that the election be held then. It may be held sooner. However, it has become custom because of the "five day" probationary period. Also, this allows the actors to become acquainted and to form some judgment as to who can best represent them as deputy. In companies where a chorus is employed there will also be a singers' deputy and a dancers' deputy, as well as the principals' deputy. The deputy must be a senior member of Equity, if one is employed in the company. If not, a junior member may serve as deputy. Stage managers do not customarily serve as deputy.

The deputy has jurisdiction over conditions of employment such as hours and safe and sanitary conditions of the theatre. While most experienced actors realize the importance of the position, less experienced actors sometimes think that it is a lot of work for no reward. The stage manager, as a fellow member of Equity, should disabuse them of this notion quickly.

The deputy has the use of the Call board for posting official Equity notices. Generally a portion of the Call board is reserved for his use.

STAGE HANDS UNION RULES

(Wardrobe personnel are included in these rules, although not always mentioned specifically. Their duties are approximately parallel to those of the other production crew heads.)

EARLY REHEARSAL PERIOD. Practically all theatres in New York City that are used for rehearsals are under the jurisdiction of the Stage Hands Union. However, no stage hand need be hired for a rehearsal, if these rules are followed:

1. LIGHTS. Only the permanent stage work lights may be used. Or, if a production is in residence, the work lights for that production.

2. SCENERY. No scenery of any type may be used. Or, if the stage has a permanent setting, no variation to it may be made.

3. PROPERTIES. Only substitute rehearsal properties may be used.

4.COSTUMES. Substitute accessories (shoes, handkerchiefs, hats, fans, pin-on trains, etc.) may be used.

5. SOUND. Substitute makeshifts may be used, e.g., a bicycle bell for a phone bell, a slapstick for a gun shot, etc.

If more elaborate facilities are required, stage hands in the proper department must be hired.

There are a few theatres (in schools, hotels, and office buildings) and many rehearsal halls (hotel ballrooms, clubrooms, etc.) that are not under the jurisdiction of the Stage Hands Union. Anything may be used in these rehearsal places. However, their inaccessibility and limited space practically eliminate utilizing elaborate rehearsal accoutrements.

The rule for marking ground plans on the stage floors of theatres under the jurisdiction of the Stage Hands Union is simple. *Only a stage hand may make such markings.* If the markings are to be made permanently on the stage floor, or temporarily on a ground cloth, using paint (oil or water color), chalk, tapes or any other method that may be devised, the threare's three house crew heads are hired to make the markings. They are hired for a minimum call. If a temporary ground cloth, marked or unmarked, is used especially for rehearsals, stage hands handle it. If ground cloths are laid before rehearsals and removed after, or transferred to another place of rehearsal, stage hands handle them.

The stage manager does not apply ground plan markings. He may make a very few temporary chalk marks to indicate doors, stairs, etc., but he must not s⁺retch the markings into elaborate plans.

However, the stage manager must have done his homework! He must know exactly what markings are to go on the stage, what colors of tape to be used, and exactly where (in terms of Upstage from the curtain line and right and left from the center line) the markings are to go.

MANUFACTURE AND HANDLING OF THE PHYSICAL PRODUCTION

The manufacture of the elements of the production is done in union shops under the supervision of the designer. The selection of ready-made articles may be made by anyone.

193

The transfer of the physical elements from the shops to the theatre, or from baggage cars to storage houses to the theatre, is handled by the Theatrical Transfer Union. Delivery is made to the door of the theatre. There the elements are received by the stage hands, and the Transfer Union's jurisdiction ends.

Once in the theatre, the elements are handled, assembled, operated and maintained by stage hands only. There is one exception for all productions—painting, repainting, or retouching of scenery is done by a member of the United Scenic Artists Local, who is known as a scenic artist or retouch man. There will be other exceptions for some productions, usually in matters of installation of special elements at the first setup. These would include special structural steelwork, elaborate draperies, complicated carpeting, linoleum laying and such things. They are installed by a specialist, usually not a stage hand. However, once installed, they are operated and maintained by stage hands.

In the theatre the elements are divided into catagories or departments and are handled by members of the proper department and not by members of other departments.

Example:

An operator (electrician) is hired to move a lighting instrument during a scenery change. This is his one and only duty. He may be utilized for other work in the Electrical Department, if such work can be found. He may not be borrowed by the Property or Carpentry Departments, even though he may be idle. If the Property or Carpentry Departments need more help, they hire more clearers and grips. The operator remains an operator and is not permitted in the other departments.

Actors and stage managers do not handle, operate or maintain the physical elements of the production, except as required by the stage action of the play. This does not mean that actors and stage managers are forbidden to touch things. It means this: actors and stage managers must not handle an element for the purpose, conscious or unconscious, of eliminating the services of a stage hand. This general rule applies: stage hands move and operate the elements, actors and stage managers may adjust them.

194

Example:

A desk, with its accessories, is carried onto the stage and set on its markings by stage hands only. The accessories on top of, or in the desk may be rearranged or adjusted by an actor or stage manager, without the help or attendance of a stage hand.

Example:

Stage managers will operate the controls of intercom systems, and of cuing systems. They will not install or maintain such systems. They will operate phone bells and other self-contained sound effects. They will not operate elaborate electronic sound equipment, unless a stage hand, otherwise unoccupied, stands by.

Costumes are handled and maintained by the Wardrobe Department. While touring, the costumes are packed by the Wardrobe Department, but the loaded trunks, hampers, boxes, are handled by the Property Department.

CLASSIFICATION OF STAGE HANDS

Stage hands may be divided into three general groups:

1. HOUSE CREW HEADS. The heads of the three departments (Carpenter, Property, Electrical) are hired by the theatre on a seasonal contract. They receive a weekly salary for the weeks a production is in residence. In New York City they must be members of Theatrical Protective Union Local #1, IATSE. There is no house Wardrobe Department.

2. PRODUCTION CREW. These are specialists, hired by the producer, who are part of the producer's staff. There may be one or more for each department, or there may be none. They are hired by contract and receive a weekly salary. Their contract is different from the house crew heads', and is known as a "road contract." Their employment is for a specific job—tryout tour, New York run, regular tour, or all three. They may be members of any IA Local in the United States or Canada.

3. CASUALS. Individual members of Local #1 (or of the local in the city where the production is playing), hired for a specific job. These jobs include loading and unloading baggage cars; taking in, setting up, taking down, putting out or working the performance of the produc-

tion; and any incidental repair or rehearsal work required. (The title used by members of the IA for these individuals is "stage hand." However, as "stage hand" is also the generic title for all members of the Stage Hands Union, "casual" is used to differentiate these individuals from house heads and production crew. These casuals may also be identified by the department to which they are assigned—car loader, grip, clearer or handler, and operator.)

WORKING HOURS

Production Crew. These men are hired on a twenty-four-a-day, seven-day-a-week basis. They receive a flat salary and get no overtime.

House Crew Heads. The house crew heads' normal working week is an eight-performance week, divided among the six days, with no more than two performances a day. In addition to working the performance, some theatre owners make arrangements with the house crew heads to be in attendance at the theatre during part of the morning and afternoon. They maintain and repair elements of the theatre structure.

The above is the normal weekly routine when a production is in residence. During the setting up and taking down, *all* of them are in attendance at all times, even though only one department may be working. The house crew heads receive overtime during these periods, if work goes beyond regular working hours.

Casuals. Casuals work by the day and by the hour, or by the performance. For the setup, take-down, and such periods, there is a regular workday of a specified number of hours. If work extends beyond the regular workday, overtime is paid. If overtime exceeds a certain number of hours, or goes beyond a certain time of day, it becomes "extra overtime."

Casuals who work a performance are paid by the performance. A regular scale is set for eight performances a week. Extra performances have another scale. The performance is limited to three and one-half hours at the regular scale. These three and one-half hours include performance preparations, and after-performance stacking, storing and cleaning up. Overtime is charged for performances that require more than three and one-half hours of work.

The term "minimum call" should be understood. It implies two things: (1) the minimum number of hands that must be used for a specified job, and (2) the minimum number of hours for which they receive payment.

Example:
A special rehearsal is to be held. Only a portion of the scenery and properties are to be used, and only work lights are needed. The full complement of hands is not needed. A minimum call is established. Minimum calls vary from job to job, from production to production, and from city to city.

BOX OFFICE

Box office treasurers are union men who have their own rules for working hours, number of men to be employed, use of the box office, etc. Moreover, they are bonded by insurance companies who also impose restrictions. In general, unauthorized persons—and that includes all actors and stage managers—are not permitted into the box office. Sometimes treasurers permit actors and stage managers to enter the box office in emergencies, such as to receive an emergency phone call. This courtesy should not be abused, and permission to make outgoing calls from the box office should not be requested. There should be no loitering around the box office.

MUSICIANS

The stage manager will have little to do with the hiring or working conditions of musicians. This is done by the contractor and the conductor. Rehearsal breaks and minimum calls will be taken care of by the contractor, although the stage manager should make it his business to co-ordinate these with the company breaks and calls.

The stage manager should also make it a part of his pre-performance checklist to see that the conductor is in the theatre and ready to go. If he is not, the stage manager should check with the assistant conductor to see that he is prepared. The company should always be informed if the assistant conductor is to conduct the performance.

Theatre employees, such as ushers, porters, cleaning women, ticket-takers, doormen and elevator operators are under the supervision of the house manager. Any contact the stage manager has with these employees should be made through the house manager.

The stage manager's contact with the stage doorman will be somewhat more direct, however. The stage doorman will be taking telephone messages, keeping tabs on who is in the theatre and directing visitors to the backstage area. It is customary for the stage manager to tip the stage doorman at the end of each week. Most managements consider this an expense account item.

Appendix E:
Off-Broadway Stage Managing

This handbook has attempted to outline the duties of a stage manager on Broadway or on tour. But (thank heavens) stage managers' employment opportunities are not limited to the Broadway theatre. Actors' Equity has different contracts for Off-Broadway, Stock, Repertory theatre, Dinner theatre and even some special contracts for specific theatre operations. The beginning stage manager may find himself stage managing an amateur theatre production or non-union Stock.

Off-Broadway will differ very little from Broadway, except that the stage hand situation will be different. The stage manager will find himself moving scenery, setting props, perhaps running the light board. In Stock companies, particularly "one-week" Stock, the problems of preparing understudies will be at a minimum—although the stage manager may find himself going on with a script in his hand! In some repertory companies the problem of keeping the company fresh will be the director's.

Obviously, the stage manager can find out what is expected of him by *a.* discussing his duties with the producer at the outset of his engagement, and *b.* a thorough reading of the union rules which apply to the particular kind of theatre.

Appendix F:
Afterword

Well, kiddies, you have plowed your way through the Gruver/ Hamilton epic, *The Stage Manager's Handbook*. Lively reading, wasn't it? Nothing in it is actually untrue (which, I suppose, can be said for very few books these days) but it bears about as much relation to Getting Ahead In Show Business as Frank Merriwell does to the life of J. Paul Getty.

For example, does it tell you how to get a job stage managing a show? No, it does not. In fact its tone implies that Blessed Are They Who Work Hard, Keep Their Scripts Clean and Lists Straight For They Shall Dine Often At Sardi's, Own Oldsmobile Station Wagons And Pretty Houses In Connecticut. Simply not true, friends! In fact, many of the fellows in the business who are intimately acquainted with the finer things of life wouldn't know a light plot if it came up and bit them in the ankle and are constantly turning to the master carpenter and saying, "Say, Harry, that little thingus on the whatchamacallit looks pretty weird. Is it supposed to look that way?"

Not that such chaps are dumb-dumbs. Indeed, they are not. It's just that while you were busy learning to keep prop plots up to date they were learning other things which fitted them more for the rough and tumble life on Broadway. An explanation of these other things is now in order.

Getting A Job: One of the terrible truths about show business is: If you aren't working, you aren't. That should read, you aren't, period! Oh, you can go around saying that you are a stage manager, director, actor, producer or what have you, but the ugly question always arises, "Where are you working?" (Usually asked by the credit department of Bloomingdale's or the Chemical Bank.) If you start to fumble or mutter something about being between engagements, the conversation is over. You can see it by the glaze that comes over the credit manager's eyes. From then on you can be witty, even hilariously droll, you can whip out your doctorate certificate from the Sorbonne, you can do a little tap dance, you can show pictures of the wife and kids, but unless said wife is Julie Harris or a member of the Kennedy Family, Buster, you've had it. You're an un-person. You don't exist. And no one in his right mind would loan you a Confederate farthing.

So the big thing is to get a job. Which is a lot easier for me, sitting drinking warmed-over coffee, to write on my Smith-Corona than it is to do. But it's not impossible, if you know the system.

William Goldman, who is a pretty sensible gent, talks about "the muscle" in any production. That is the person in any production without whom the money cannot be raised, nor the Shuberts induced to provide a theatre for the show. This can be the producer, star, director and even occasionally, the author. These muscular folk are also responsible for the hiring and firing of stage managers. If, for example, George Abbott, Joe Hardy or Mike Nichols is engaged to direct a play, he might say to the General Manager, "Oh, Bill Fotheringay always stage manages for me." Bill Fotheringay becomes a person and the Credit Manager of Bloomingdale's learns to love him.

On the other hand, one of the above esteemed gentlemen of the theatre might say, "Stage Manager? Oh, hell, I don't care so long as he speaks English." Now in this situation it is a pretty sound wager that someone (say the author or star) has already approached the General Manager and said something like, "Listen, if Mike (or Joe or Mr. Abbott) doesn't have a regular stage manager, I'd like you to think about my friend, Hector Jones." The General Manager, who is engaged at this point of the production in "keeping everybody happy" does, indeed, think about Hector Jones. He calls Hector in for an interview. (Of which, more later.)

What the "muscle" in the above case has done, in effect, is to turn the problem of hiring a stage manager over to the "assistant muscle." You may be thinking at this point, "Ah, me, what chance have I, the honor graduate from Oneida College of Dramatic Art, to crack this tightly knit circle of muscles and assistant muscles?" And you're right up to a point. But all is not hopeless. There is a chance and it occurs when the muscle surrenders his prerogative to the assistant muscle.

Now, everybody usually knows who the muscle is in a production. (A notable exception may have occured when David Merrick hired Jackie Gleason for a show. They both considered themselves the muscle and the results must have been pyrotechnic.) But the position of assistant muscle is never clear and may have three or four candidates, all campaigning furiously for the job. This often gets right down to the secretaries and office boys and is known as "internal politics," which proves that show business is not really very different in some respects from IBM or General Motors. At any event, when B has discovered that A has suggested Hector Jones, B realizes that A is campaigning for the office of assistant muscle. And to be in the running, he, too, has to have a candidate for stage manager. You're in luck when you have been at a party the night before and met the office boy and discovered he used to date your sister. He *has* to have a suggestion and you seemed like an affable chap to him and he knows you're a stage manager and out of work. So your name gets thrown into the hopper and you too will probably be interviewed by the General Manager. Your chances aren't as good as the producer's brother or even the fellow who's dating the designer's assistant, but you're at least at the convention and your name is in nomination. If you're a devotee of American Political Conventions you know that the damnedest things happen. (Who *was* Alfred Landon?) You also can see, I am sure, that the issue will be decided on something quite different from your ability to make a smashing prop plot. The first thing that will happen to you, in this hypothetical case will be:

The Interview. The interview will be conducted by the General Manager. About the only thing the General Manager wants to know is if you really do speak English, as advertised. He will also discover at this interview whether you speak theatre-ese. Not that it's important that you do—remember, your talents or lack thereof won't mean very much at this point—but your name has been placed in nomination and you need all the votes you can get. The General Manager, just possibly, may not be running for the office of assistant muscle or his candidate for stage manager may have popped the director in the eye on the last show. At any rate, it won't hurt to sling a little theatre-ese at him. Theatre-ese isn't very hard to learn. Sitting around any one of a dozen theatrical restaurants with alert ears should give you the hang of it in a few weeks.

It consists mostly in how you describe your own activities. For example, you may be asked what your last show was. You answer this, not according to what your last show was, but what *kind* of show your last show was. If your last show was a big hit, say, *Fiddler*, you look the General Manager straight in the eye and say, "I was Production Stage Manager of *Fiddler On The Roof*, directed all the road companies and also companies in London, Paris, Israel and Montevideo."

And then, shut up! You're winning. You have just said the magic words in show business. Your last show was a big hit. And as everybody knows, the stage manager who stage manages one hit will stage manage another. These things have a way of repeating themselves. The General Manager will stutter and stammer a bit (he probably never had a hit as big as *Fiddler*) and consider you a very respectable person. You have just passed the producer's brother and the assistant designer's boy friend. You've got a very good chance.

If, on the other hand, your last show was a complete stinkeroo which lasted two nights, you phrase it a little differently. You say, "Well, last season, I helped Gadg bring in *Adam's Off Ox*." This phraseology implies several things. First, that you know Gadg well enough to call him "Gadg." Which puts you in the very select company of about 85,000 actors, stage managers, producers, press agents, stage doormen, bartenders, cab drivers and *Daily News* readers. Nobody (except possibly his milkman) calls him Mr. Kazan, and the last person to call him Elia was probably his mother. But it *is* theatre-ese, and that's the whole point.

It also implies that Gadg came to you, knelt and kissed your ring and begged you to help him out. That he wouldn't have done the show without you (which may have been a good thing, considering that two-night run, but don't mention that). And that you, knowing all the while that the show was slated to close on Thursday, couldn't resist Gadg's charm and blandishments and made a huge sacrifice and did the show. (Let's face it, what Gadg really said was, "Oh, hell, I don't care, so long as he speaks English.")

It may be that your own past activities may not hold up under scrutiny. Possibly your only experience on the Big Apple was a two-night stint as second assistant stage manager of *Adam's Off Ox*. (You never said you were the stage manager, remember?) After you pull the

208

line about helping Gadg,—and say it with a sad little put-upon smile that seems to forgive Gadg for messing up your season and not listening to you—you start on the offensive. Something like, "I can't visualize the set. Who's doing it?" (This shows him that you have studied the play, but, with charming modesty, you don't know more than the designer.)

Now right here we better introduce you to the eighth beatitude. "Judge not, lest Ye go out on a limb." Remembering this will get you through all sorts of ticklish situations. For example:

You have just asked who is to design the show. The General Manager will say, "Oliver." (Or Jo, or David or Peter—only to the outside world do designers have last names; inside the business, you're supposed to *know*.) Now the chances are that the General Manager has just had a hell of a battle on the telephone with Oliver (or Jo, or David or Peter) about the designer's fee, the cost of the set or some such trivia. On the other hand, they may have had lunch together an hour ago and Oliver (or Jo, or David or Peter) has picked up the check. So you say, "It should be right down his alley. His stuff is so interesting." And you're covered all the way. You haven't said his stuff was good, nor have you said it was bad. You've said interesting. A great little old word that fits, pro or con, any theatrical conversation. You've also said it *should* be right down his alley. Can you help it if he messes it up?

This interview will end with the General Manager saying something about letting you know and calling you to set up an appointment with the director. And you will go away and the political wheels will continue to turn.

It is entirely possible that the General Manager will, indeed, call you to set up an appointment with the director. If he does, the call will come about thirty-six hours after you have given up hope of receiving it.

The Interview With The Director. About the only thing the Director really wants to know is if you really do speak English. Oh, the General Manager will have told him so, but, you see, very few General Managers really speak English and most Directors know this. So he will want to find out for himself.

The interview will start off pretty much the same way the other one did. Not that it's particularly relevant or that anyone really cares what other shows you've done, but nobody has ever figured out any other method of beginning a theatrical interview. So you'll follow the script as in the first interview. (Except, if the Director is Gadg, himself. Then you won't be able to use that line about helping Gadg. You'll have to change it to Teak, or Stash or Mr. Abbott.)

One big *DON'T* for this interview. Don't, under any circumstances, ask about his plans for directing the play. He has been pretty busy lately directing other plays, doing movies in Hollywood, having lunch with his agent, or quarreling with the General Manager about his fee or the fact that he wants Oliver Thrumb for the role of the janitor and Mr. Thrumb is asking an outrageous salary. So he probably hasn't figured out himself what he plans to do with it.

A good thing to talk with directors about is their last show. Even if it was a flop. You adored it. And you don't think most audiences understood what he was driving at. (*That's* why it closed after three days.) You see, he feels that way, too—he *can't* believe that he did a lousy job. And when he finds out that you thought it was marvelous, you will rise way above Clive Barnes and John Simon in his estimation. Which may not be exactly the top of the heap, but you're on the right road.

You will be able to tell from the way the interview ends how good your chances are. If he says, "Well, we'll let you know Sam," and your name is Claude, forget it. Get a job at Brentano's and put the kids in public school. If, however, he says, "I'll have the General Manager call you. By the way, give me your telephone number, Claude," you can take your wife out to dinner that night with a moderately good conscience.

Money. At some point you will discuss money with a poor, shrivelled, old man on the brink of poverty and starvation. This will be the General Manager. Some of the finest acting in the theatre is done by General Managers discussing fiscal problems. Remember that Burbage was a manager and probably learned to play Lear discussing salary with a stage manager. If you start out by saying, "Well, I'd like to have three-fifty," and then wax eloquent about the kids' dental work and the pressure on you from Bloomingdale's, you'll wind up getting three hundred. A simple but effective tactic is what I like to call the 29c a pound approach. You start by asking yourself, "What's the price of carrots?" Then you answer yourself, "Twenty-nine cents a pound." Do this several times. Then, in exactly the same tone of voice say, "Four hundred and fifty." Practice this exercise at home and then when you get into the General Managers office and he asks you what your salary is, think just for a split second of the "29c a pound" inflection, and say, "Four hundred and fifty." The matter-of-fact quality of your voice will allow him no point on which to debate and he may even forget to feign the heart attack that he was planning. One little caution, however. Don't get nervous and say, "Twenty-nine cents a pound". You won't get it and he'll only think you're a damned fool idiot.

Keeping The Job. So you have gotten the job. You haven't auditioned by throwing some sample cues, you haven't laid out a rehearsal stage on spec, you have merely been affable and spoken English and a little theatre-ese. Besides the producer's brother is in the hospital with a gall bladder operation and the designer's assistant and her friend have had a hell of a fight.

The first thing the stage manager must think about is keeping the job he has just gotten. If the show is a hit, this is no problem. Everybody loves everybody in a hit and everybody's job is secure, as long as he doesn't do something unpardonable, like being rude to the producer's wife.

The question is, how do you tell early in the game if the show is to be a hit? Fairly simple! If you can read the script straight through and chuckle at the funny parts and cry at the sad parts and not fall asleep or become impatient, if the music and lyrics amuse and delight you and don't sound too familiar, if the director sounds as if he's living in *this* world, if the star is someone *you'd* pay ten bucks to go see, if the producer is David Merrick, you've got hold of a good thing. Operate on the hit psychology. Do your job well. Be nice to everyone. And rest assured, your telephone will ring for years to come—other producers wanting you to stage manage their shows, for as everyone in show business knows, it is the stage manager who makes a show a hit.

But let's face it, dear friends, in the above situation it is Bill Fotheringay who is the stage manager, and his price is 37c a pound without batting an eye.

Keeping the job on a flop show (or "non-hit," as we like to call them) is a bit more complicated. If you get a terrible headache while reading the second act and discreet inquiries are met with the intelligence that "The Boys" are putting together a new second act before rehearsals begin (in show business all authors are known as "The Boys." They can be Irving Berlin, Noel Coward and Lillian Hellman, with a combined experience of 173 years, they are still "The Boys."), if the music and lyrics are Tchaikovsky and Mother Goose, if the director is a "genius," if the star is a 1940's Hollywood retread, if the producer is your brother, you've got the makings of a disaster. It will demand all your piety and wit to stay on after the Boston opening.

You may ask, at this point, why should you want to stay on after the Boston opening, if the show is such a bomb. Let me put it this way: Six weeks of rehearsal, six weeks out of town, two weeks of previews, and open and close in one week. A total of fifteen weeks. At $450 per week: $6,750. Bloomingdale's will be very grateful.

Why should it be such a ticklish task keeping the job on a "non-hit" show, he asked, rhetorically. Well, you see, in every non-hit show there is a goat. Or goats. A person, or persons who are directly responsible that the audience sat in stony silence through the comedy scenes and giggled at the death scene in Philadelphia. It can be anyone. "The whole gag would have worked if she'd been wearing yellow slippers instead of blue slippers," says the director. And the wardrobe mistress has a good cry, packs her bag, and returns to New York. "If he stages it behind a tree, how can anybody see it, much less laugh," says the author. And the director calls his agent and tells him to take the Hollywood deal. He's on his way.

In short, the panic is on. An out-of-town tryout can be unfavorably compared to the French Directoire or the McCarthy Era. With a little

212

Inquisition thrown in. And everybody is vulnerable, including stage managers.

There are a few rules for staying out of the line of fire. First: Look busy! Most people don't really know what a stage manager does. It's like the Secretary of Commerce. Everybody knows that a show needs a stage manager, just as they know that the Government has to have a Secretary of Commerce, but nine out of ten people would be hard pressed to explain the duties of either. Then, too, most people get their impressions of stage managers from movies of the thirties. In those films he was always a harried looking guy (ably played by Elisha Cook, Jr.) who walked around with a clip-board looking over-worked, under-paid, disheveled and worried. It's useless to try to explain to anyone that 40% of your time is spent waiting for someone else to make a decision, 30% listening to bootless discussions about a scene that's going to be cut anyway, and 10% in the men's room taking tran-quilizers. A good system is to come in each morning dressed to the nines. After a half-hour, remove your jacket; after the second half-hour, loosen your tie; after the third, roll up your sleeves; after the fourth, muss your hair a little; etc. At the end of the day you should look utterly exhausted and everyone will say you're a hell of a stage manager.

Second: Never do anything right the first time! Remember that kid in high school who got nothing but D's and F's until his Senior year, when he came through with a solid C average? And remember, too, you'd have thought he had just won the Nobel Prize. Teachers, parents, all thought he was the cat's pajamas. While you, poor devil, cracked straight A's, but in your Senior year fell to a B-plus average. Your parents talked of disowning you or sending you to apprentice in an abatoir. It's the same way in show business, chums. Do it right the first time, and the one time you blow it, the Company Manager will have your train ticket back to New York in his pocket. Do it wrong a time or two first, and that becomes par for the course. You're covered.

Third: Remember the Eighth Beatitude. Never, never, never go out on a limb. For example: someone comes up to you and says, "What do you think of the new scene, Claude?"

If you say, "Gee Whiz, I think it's a real swell scene," you're in trouble. If you listen carefully, you can almost hear it echoing throughout the theatre. "Claude loves the new scene." "Claude thinks the new scene is great." "Claude says the new scene is going to save the show." In a peculiar kind of way it becomes "Claude's scene." When the scene dies an ugly death on stage in performance, Claude becomes the idiot who is directly responsible for the failure of the entire show. Sorry, Bloomingdale's. What you should have said was, "It's interesting. I hope they can make it work." That great old omnibus word "interesting" again. But the real heart of the matter here is that word, "they." Whoever you're talking to, will interpret the "they" the way he wants to. If it's the director, "they" will mean the actors, whom he will, of course blame if the scene lays an egg. And you have tacitly agreed with him by putting the onus on "them" to make it work. You will be his friend. If you're talking to an actor, "they" will mean the author and director and again, you are on his side. If it's the author, "they" will be the director and actors, and it's always wise to get in good with authors. If you're talking to the producer, "they" will be everyone else but himself and his loyal, brave, courteous, helpful, true, wise and employed stage manager.

Finally:

How To Get The Next Job. We might as well face the fact. This turkey you're with is going to fold very close to the time it opens. And who is going to pay the rent and/or Saks Fifth Avenue for that dazzling dress your wife bought for the opening? The time to begin angling for that next job is *now*. And how do you do this? Just remember, today's goat may be tomorrow's muscle. For instance: While you're helping the director pack to go back to New York because he staged the big comic scene behind a tree, drop in a little comment, like, "Gee, Harry, they really screwed you good. Your concept was the only way this show could have worked. For two cents I'd leave myself." (Make sure the place isn't bugged first.) He won't take you up on your last proposal— directors hate to part with any amount of money—but he will feel that you are perhaps the only person who understands his true genius. And if he ever gets another show, he is quite likely to say, "Oh, Claude

214

Grayton always stage manages for me." Naturally, the next day while talking to the producer about the director's departure, you say, "Now that Scrunch (or if he's English—Peter. Most English directors are Peters) has gone, I think we have a real chance. He was a nice fellow, but just didn't seem to understand this show." That was precisely what the producer said when firing Scrunch (or Peter) and he will think you a hell of a fellow for agreeing with him in such a loyal, brave, courteous, helpful, true, wise and employed manner. Similar remarks can be made to and about the departing authors, actors, stage hands, composers, designers and stage managers (if you happen to be the assistant stage manager).

You may feel that there is a certain amount of opportunistic, two-faced, double-dealing here. And I cannot help but agree. But this is show business, Baby, where Darwin's Law applies to the nth power.

I hope and trust that these few little hints will help you attain a position of affluence and happiness in show business. I wish you the greatest success.